Winning The War On Drugs:
To Legalise or Not?

RICHARD STEVENSON

*Director of Health Economics and
Lecturer, Department of Economics,
University of Liverpool*

With Commentaries by

JULIUS MERRY

and

PETER REUTER,
MICHAEL FARRELL
and JOHN STRANG

Published by
INSTITUTE OF ECONOMIC AFFAIRS
1994
SECOND IMPRESSION 1997

First published in March 1994
Second Impression October 1997

THE INSTITUTE OF ECONOMIC AFFAIRS
2 Lord North Street, Westminster,
London SW1P 3LB

Hobart Paper 124

ISSN 0073-2818

ISBN 0-255 36330-3

Printed in Great Britain by
OPTICHROME THE PRINTING GROUP, WOKING, SURREY
Set in Baskerville 11 on 12 point

CONTENTS

LIST OF FIGURES:

FOREWORD

'Wars' on drugs seem everywhere to be in progress, both in countries which produce drugs and in those where the consumption habit seems to have assumed dangerous proportions. In order to promote discussion of this important issue, the Institute of Economic Affairs commissioned Richard Stevenson, Director of the Health Economics Unit at Liverpool University to write a paper, from an economist's viewpoint, on the drugs problem and what remedies there might be.

Mr Stevenson's paper, which constitutes the main part of Hobart Paper 124, begins (Chapter I) by reviewing historical experience of attempts to deal with drugs problems in Britain and abroad. In Chapters II and III Stevenson turns to the case for prohibition, arguing that neither on paternalistic nor on market failure grounds can a case be made for prohibition: indeed, in his view, prohibition *creates* external costs in terms of gangsterism, corruption and law enforcement costs. It is '...wrong in principle and does not work in practice'.

Chapter IV discusses some alternatives to the 'Drug War' which Stevenson argues have '...advantages over prohibition' though '...most represent easements of policy as it applies to users rather than dealers'. However, he believes a better approach is legalisation of drugs which '...deals directly with the fundamental problem which is to wrest control of drug markets from criminals'.

In the most controversial part of his paper (Chapters V and VI), Mr Stevenson sets out a positive and detailed case for legalisation '...as a response to drug problems which offers substantial social savings and deals directly and swiftly with criminality'. It would no longer be an offence to possess drugs, to use them or to trade in them but drugs would carry a health warning and sales to children would remain illegal.

The case Mr Stevenson presents is not the mainstream view in Britain but, as he says, prohibition is losing support

'...among people who deal directly with drug problems', including judges and senior policemen.

Mr Stevenson's advocacy of legalisation is coupled with a warning against dogmatism. 'It would be sensible to proceed cautiously, to monitor consequences and to revise ideas in response to experience.' Legalisation will not 'solve all drug problems' but those which remain will be social and medical. Users, their families, voluntary agencies and doctors '...will cope better in a legal system where problems are visible'.

In the interests of balanced discussion, the Institute asked some eminent medical practitioners with long experience of dealing with drug-related problems to write commentaries on Mr Stevenson's paper.

Professor Julius Merry of St. Thomas's Hospital and the University of Surrey is broadly in agreement with Mr Stevenson, whose paper he describes as 'balanced and wide-ranging'. Professor Merry explains the history of narcotic addiction, starting with China which '...was the first country where opium presented a social problem'. In his view, events are moving ahead of legislation and it is now time to '...accept the logic of some form of legalisation'.

The 'war on drugs' has failed in Merry's view. Although there is '...no hard evidence that legalisation would reduce the size of the drug problem', it would

> '...certainly dramatically reduce illegal profits from drugs and would undoubtedly reduce criminal involvement. It would also ensure that addicts received quality-controlled heroin without feeling that they were being forced to indulge in criminal or anti-social activities'.

Coupled with legalisation there should be more resources:

> '...directed to the education of the public – especially young people – in the pernicious and serious dangers of all drugs, including alcohol and tobacco'.

In a second commentary, Professor Peter Reuter (Department of Criminology, University of Maryland), Dr Michael Farrell and Dr John Strang (National Addiction Centre, Institute of Psychiatry, London) disagree strongly with Stevenson. Their contention is that '...drug control is far more complicated than Richard Stevenson's analysis suggests. Consequently we are more than doubtful whether

[8]

legalisation would in fact be a net benefit to society'. In their view, supply-side policies have had more impact than Stevenson allows.

Moreover, they argue that legalisation might significantly increase drug consumption. The example they use is that, even if a number equal to only one-quarter of those now suffering long-term damage from alcohol consumption were to become heroin addicts, the number of heroin users in the United States would be five times what it is now. Because psychoactive drugs free people from their inhibitions, a 'much expanded user base might lead to more crime, though of a different kind from that found under current prohibitions'.

Reuter *et al.* are concerned also about the irreversibility of legalisation. If legalisation resulted in much increased drug abuse it would, they claim, be hard to revert to prohibition. They favour alternatives which '...lie between tough prohibition and legalisation', such as needle exchange programmes, concentration by the police on 'disorderly markets' or those which provide drugs to new users, and more flexible sentencing policies. They conclude:

> '...if the choice is between prohibition and the speculative gains of legalisation...more thought about how to reduce the costs of prohibition is what ought to take precedence on a realistic policy research agenda'.

The views expressed in Hobart Paper 124 on this controversial issue are those of the authors, not of the Institute (which has no corporate view), its Trustees, Advisers or Directors. The *Paper* is published as an aid to discussion on how best to deal with this particularly serious social problem.

March 1994   COLIN ROBINSON
Editorial Director, Institute of Economic Affairs;
Professor of Economics, University of Surrey

THE AUTHORS

RICHARD STEVENSON is the Director of the Health Economics Unit and a lecturer in the Department of Economics at Liverpool University. A graduate of the LSE and Stanford University, he has held visiting appointments in the United States, and has researched and published in many areas of health economics. An interest in drugs stemmed from concern for the welfare of addicts, and a long-standing interest in the economics of neonatal intensive care for low birthweight infants, some of whom are born addicted to drugs. Current work concerns diabetes, low-back pain, a follow-up study of low birthweight infants, and the economic theory of drug addiction.

Richard Stevenson's publications on the drugs issue include 'The economics of drug policy', in *Policies and Prescribing: The British System of Drug Control* (Macmillan, 1991); 'Can markets cope with drugs?', in the *Journal of Drug Issues* (Vol.20, No.4, 1990); and 'Legalisation in Practice', in *Modern Medicine of Australia* (September 1991).

DR JULIUS MERRY is Visiting Professor of Clinical Psychiatry at the University of Surrey, and an Honorary Physician in Psychological Medicine at St. Thomas's Hospital, London. He was previously Consultant Psychiatrist at St. Thomas's and St. George's Hospitals, London (1956-88), and Consultant Psychiatrist in charge of the Alcohol Dependency Unit, Epsom, Surrey (1956-88).

His clinical interests are in social psychiatry, therapeutic communities, and alcohol and drug dependency. He has published widely on the subjects of social psychiatry, and the biochemical and endocrinological aspects of alcohol and drug dependency, with papers in the *British Journal of Addiction, The Lancet,* the *British Medical Journal* and the *British Journal of Psychiatry.*

JOHN STRANG is Getty Senior Lecturer in the Addictions and Deputy Director of the Addiction Research Unit at the National Addiction Centre (Institute of Psychiatry/The Maudsley) where he is also a Consultant Psychiatrist in drug dependence. He is adviser (drugs) to the Department of Health, a member of the Expert Advisory Group on AIDS and the Advisory Council on the Misuse of Drugs. His interests include analysis of policy issues and the drugs/AIDS relationship and he is particularly involved in recent study of changes in route of use of heroin and cocaine.

MICHAEL FARRELL is a Senior Lecturer and Consultant Psychiatrist at the National Addiction Centre (Institute of Psychiatry/The Maudsley). Formerly Senior Medical Officer on Alcohol and Drugs, Department of Health. He is responsible for a large Community Drug Service. He is a working member of the AIDS and Drug Misuse Working Party on Prevention to the Advisory Council on the Misuse of Drugs. His interests include drug misuse in the young, national and international drug control policies and research on provision of drug services.

PETER REUTER is a Professor in the School of Public Affairs and in the Department of Criminology at the University of Maryland. From 1989 to 1993 he was Co Director of the Drug Policy Research Center at the RAND Corporation. His initial research dealt with the organisation of illegal markets. Since 1985 his research has been concerned with drug policy, particularly the effectiveness of alternative drug enforcement strategies.

ACKNOWLEDGEMENTS

Nicholas Dorn, John Marks, Russell Newcombe and colleagues who preferred to remain anonymous, have contributed valuable comments. Their advice was all the more generous since they do not necessarily share the views expressed.

R.S.

AUTHOR'S INTRODUCTION

And that singular anomaly, the Prohibitionist —
I don't think he'll be missed —
I'm sure he'll not be missed.

W.S. Gilbert (*The Mikado*)

This paper argues for the legalisation of all drugs currently prohibited in UK and international law. The drugs act on the central nervous system and are known collectively as 'mind-altering' or psychoactive substances. They include heroin, cocaine, crack, amphetamines, cannabis and most other commonly abused drugs. Some are addictive and most can be dangerous.

Proponents of drug legalisation know the danger of drug use and wish to reduce it. Legal prohibition makes drug use more dangerous than it need be and hands the control of drug markets to criminals. Where drug problems ramify into gangsterism, corruption and political violence, they are caused not so much by illegal drugs as by illegal drug money.

President Nixon declared war on drugs in 1973. Since then drug use has increased despite the expenditure of billions of pounds on law enforcement. Indeed, it is hard to escape the conclusion that most drug problems are the entirely predictable result of an attempt to 'buck the market' in one of the world's most valuable and profitable traded goods. It cannot be shown that current policy will never work, but no one believes that victory in the drug war is imminent, or that it will be cheap.

In the meantime drug problems are urgent, so it seems reasonable to seek alternatives to current policies which may be cheaper and more effective. Many possibilities exist; most fall short of full legalisation. Some are discussed in Chapter IV. All deserve serious consideration, but they do not strike directly at what many see as the central problem which is to wrest drug markets from the control of criminals.

One of the principal attractions of legalisation is that it would allow society to regain control over the production and distribution of drugs. Many sorts of legal systems are feasible.

[13]

Drugs could be produced and sold by a state monopoly but, to an economist inclined to view current drug policy as a prime example of government failure, it is natural to wonder whether a market solution might not be preferable.

This paper argues that drugs could be bought and sold in much the same way as most other goods. They would be produced by private firms, and be available, without prescription, from normal sorts of retail outlets, such as chemist's shops. Users would choose from a range of products of certified purity in much the same way that drinkers choose between beer, wine and spirits. The only restrictions would preclude sales to children, and might affect some aspects of marketing strategies such as packaging.

In this legal system, users would become more visible and amenable to advice. Some of the worst hazards of drug use would be avoided, but problems would remain. Government and voluntary agencies would retain an important rôle in treatment, education and other strategies to reduce drug-related harm. It is also suggested that some part of the social savings from legalisation should be directed to improvements in social and medical services for drug users.

The case for the legalisation of drugs has much in common with the case for legal abortion. Abortion is tragic, but given that it will occur in any circumstances, it is better that it should be performed competently. In the same way, it would be better if everyone could cope without mind-altering drugs, but prohibition is unenforceable. If some people insist on using drugs, it is better that they should buy them from law-abiding businessmen rather than criminals, and better still if they can be integrated into society and brought under medical supervision if it is needed.

Legalisation will not solve all drug problems, but the problems which remain will be medical and social rather than political and economic. Drug abuse will be less likely to impose costs on third parties (which include the tax payer) and, perhaps most importantly, legalisation is the surest and most administratively parsimonious means of 'Getting gangsters out of drugs'.[1] Criminals love prohibition. They would hate legalisation.

November 1993   RICHARD STEVENSON

---

1 *The Economist,* 2 April 1988.

I. DRUG PROBLEMS:
ORIGINS AND NATURE

Historical Perspective

The possession of and trade in opiates, cocaine and cannabis first became criminal offences in Britain under the provisions of the Dangerous Drugs Act of 1920. Previously opiates were readily available and very widely used. The sale of opium was reserved to pharmacists in 1868, but preparations containing opium were unregulated. Opiates were among the drugs most frequently prescribed by doctors, and the principal active ingredient in scores of household remedies.

The addictive potential of opiates was well known in the 19th century but opiates were, and remain, a most effective class of drugs for the relief of pain. Since the poorer classes seldom received medical attention, addiction acquired as a side-effect of medical treatment was a scourge mainly of the affluent. The recreational and experimental use of drugs was fashionable in literary circles, and pockets of addicts in East Anglia consumed enormous quantities of opium to ease the aches and pains of agricultural labour. Some of these rural addicts lived to such great age that the association between opium addiction and longevity was a subject of scientific Inquiry.

Berridge and Edwards have argued that so long as addiction was confined to specialised communities and the middle classes, addiction was not a serious social issue.[1] Pressure to legislate came from opposition to the Indo-Chinese opium trade and concern over widespread opiate use amongst the poorest classes. In particular, the public was outraged by a spate of infant deaths from overdoses of preparations of opium – soothing syrups – commonly administered to infants.

---

1 Virginia Berridge and Griffith Edwards, *Opium and the People: Opiate Use in Nineteenth-Century England*, London: Allen Lane, 1981.

A powerful anti-opium movement failed narrowly to persuade parliament to outlaw the trade in the 1880s. In the 1890s prohibitionists lobbied successfully for a Royal Commission which reported in 1895. The Report of the Opium Commission concluded that opium use had scant moral or physical adverse effects.[2] The much more powerful opium derivatives, morphine and heroin, were not widely known outside medical circles, and their use was not then a social problem. Cocaine addiction was also very rare, and cannabis was mainly of medical interest in the treatment of morphine addiction.

The Report of the Opium Commission coincided with an unexplained decline in the use of opiates, and the prohibition movement might have foundered in Britain had it not been for American initiatives. From the first international drug conference at Shanghai in 1909 to the present day, US governments have placed drug issues high on the agenda in their dealings with the rest of the world. Under the auspices of the League of Nations and the United Nations, an elaborate framework of international law has been created to suppress the trade in and the use of psychoactive substances. In all instances, UK drug law has been strengthened to comply with international treaty obligations rather than to combat British drug problems.[3]

The cornerstone of international drug law is the 1961 United Nations Single Convention on Narcotic Drugs which replaced all earlier treaties dealing with opiates, cannabis, and cocaine. In 1971 controls were extended to cover a wider range of substances to include LSD, amphetamines, barbiturates and some tranquillisers. The UK fulfils its international obligations through the Misuse of Drugs Act 1971 and a body of related law. The most recent addition is the Drug Trafficking Act 1986, which allows the courts to seize the assets of persons convicted of drug offences. Under the Misuse of Drugs Act controlled substances are listed in schedules according to toxicity, addictiveness and the perceived severity of the social problems which result from non-medical use. Maximum penalties are graded according

---

2 Parliamentary Papers, Vol.XLII: *Reports, and Minutes of Evidence of the Royal Commission on Opium*, 1895.

3 P. Bean, T*he Social Control of Drugs*, London: Martin Robertson, 1974.

to the type of drug involved, and are greater for trafficking than for possession.[4]

Global Issues

During 70 years of prohibition, drug use increased slowly until the 1960s, and then rapidly. Some (unverifiable) estimates suggest that there may now be as many as 40 million heroin addicts in the world. This growth in drug use has not been fully explained. No doubt many factors were at work, but prohibition created the illegal industry which bears much of the responsibility.

Perhaps the plainest indictment of prohibition is found in countries where drug use is traditional. In Hong Kong, Thailand and Laos, centuries of experience created conditions in which opium use was contained and controlled by custom and manners at very low social cost. In response to international pressure, anti-opium laws were enacted in these three countries in the 1950s, 1960s and 1970s. The result was the emergence of an illegal heroin industry which rapidly corrupted enforcement agencies. *Within months*, by a sort of Gresham's Law, potent drugs drove out the relatively benign. Traders promoted heroin, which is less bulky and more profitable than opium, so that opium became difficult to obtain. Addiction increased and health problems soon became acute.[5]

The effect of Western-imposed drug laws has been identical in Andean countries where coca leaves have traditionally been chewed or made into beverages. Cocaine is replacing coca; a cottage industry has been taken over by big business and addiction rates are rising dramatically.

Prohibition is responsible for only a part of the increase in drug use, but it is responsible for all of the evils generated by illegal drug money. Illegal drugs are said to rank with oil and armaments as one of the world's most valuable and profitable traded commodities. A small number of criminal firms launder tax-free sums in excess of $100 billion annually, and perhaps one-tenth of the deposits on the London money

---

4 Institute for the Study of Drug Dependence, *The Misuse of Drugs Act Explained*, London: ISDD, Hatton Garden, 1986.

5 Joseph Westermeyer, 'The pro-heroin effects of anti-opium laws in Asia', *Archives of General Psychiatry*, Vol.33, September 1976, pp.1,135-39.

market are derived from the drug trade. These frequently quoted best guesses of the scale of the illegal drug trade are unverifiable, but no one doubts that the trade is large enough to be of major international significance.

In Lebanon, Peru, Afghanistan, Laos, Cambodia and Thailand drug profits have fuelled armed insurrection. In Colombia, judges, ministers and three presidential candidates have been murdered. Elsewhere, whole governments and law enforcement agencies have been suborned by drug traders. Policemen are killed in many countries, and in the United States half of all murders are drug-related. In much of Asia, South and North America and some parts of Europe, the drug trade is closely associated with organised crime and terrorism. As Milton Friedman has put it, all of the atrocities associated with the illegal drug trade occur because the United States and other Western countries pass anti-drug laws which they cannot enforce.[6]

Illegal Drug Use in the UK

By comparison with much of the rest of the world, British drug problems might seem almost mild. Fears that American style gangsterism could spread to the UK appear to have been exaggerated. Nevertheless, fears continue. In April 1991, in the wake of violence in Manchester, the Chief Constable of Lancashire warned of the association between drug trafficking and serious crime.[7] Since then, several policemen have been killed. Traffickers are increasingly likely to carry firearms and Manchester ambulancemen have been issued with bullet-proof vests.[8]

Yet large criminal 'families' do not compete violently for drug market share, as they do in other countries. Politicians have never been implicated in drug dealing and, although a

---

6 Milton Friedman and Thomas Szasz, *On Liberty and Drugs: Essays on the Free Market and Prohibition*, ed. by A.S. Trebach and K.B. Zeese, Washington DC: The Drug Policy Foundation Press, 1992.

7 Terry Kirby, 'Drug Gangs Fight for Power in the Cities', *The Independent*, 18 April 1991.

8 *World in Action*, 'Homicide UK', Granada Television, 21 February 1994. Also 'Crack "turf wars" sweep Britain', *Today*, 23 October 1993; 'Murdered PC praised as public's unsung hero', *Evening Standard*, 27 October 1993; 'Yardie gangs raise stakes for policing', *The European*, 28 October 1993.

few cases come to light each year, police corruption is not thought to be widespread. There are no grounds for complacency, but so far Britain has avoided the nastiest features of the international drug trade. Drug problems in the UK, although serious, are mostly connected with health issues and drug-related acquisitive crime.

The extent of drug abuse in the UK is difficult to assess, not only because it is clandestine, but because many substances are involved, and the frequency of use varies widely, from occasional to weekend and daily use. Statistics on the incidence and prevalence of drug use are not collected on a routine basis, so estimates have to be made from indirect evidence.

The Home Office maintains a register of drug dependent people, notified as such by medical practitioners. Between 1991 and 1992, the number of notified addicts rose from 20,820 to 24,703, a 19 per cent increase.[9] Within these figures, the number of new addicts increased by 21 per cent to 9,700. Other indicators include arrests and convictions for drug offences. In 1991, 47,616 persons were dealt with for drug offences. Drug trafficking offences accounted for less than 3,000 cases. The commonest offence by far was the unlawful possession of cannabis (38,457 cases).[10]

Statistics on Customs and Excise seizures are another rough guide to trends in drug use. The figures are strongly influenced by the intensity and efficiency of law enforcement, but increased seizures combined with rises in all other indices leave little doubt that the illegal drug market continues to grow.

Notification figures and criminal statistics identify drug users who are desperate, indiscreet or unlucky. Large numbers of other illegal drug users do not come to the attention of the legal or medical authorities. Wide regional variations exist, but community studies suggest that notification figures underestimate the true extent of opiate dependency by a factor of between five and 10.[11] Applying

---

9 Home Office, *Statistics of Drug Addicts Notified to the Home Office, United Kingdom, 1992*, London: HMSO, May 1993.

10 Home Office, *Statistics on Drug Seizures and Offenders Dealt With, UK 1991*, London: HMSO, 1992.

11 R.L. Hartnoll, R. Lewis, M. Mitcheson, and S. Bryer, 'Estimating the prevalence of opioid dependence', *The Lancet*, 26 January 1985.

these factors to the 1992 notification figures puts the number of dependent users in the range 125,000 to 250,000. Some of the most recent increase in notifications may be explained by increased efforts to attract more addicts into treatment, but the mid-point estimate of approximately 185,000 is generally accepted as fairly reliable.[12]

Far greater numbers of people use illegal drugs frequently or occasionally without becoming dependent in any medical sense. Two of the most commonly used illegal drugs, cannabis and MDMA ('ecstasy'), are not closely associated with serious dependency problems. Even opiate use does not necessarily lead to addiction. Opiate use which is occasional or well managed is reported frequently in community studies. Far less is known about the extent of cocaine and 'crack' use, but all indicators suggest that it has increased rapidly in recent years.

A national survey conducted by Gallup and published in December 1992 concluded that the number of under 25s in Britain who have taken drugs had doubled between 1989 and 1992. The survey found that three out of 10 young people aged 15-24 admitted to taking drugs (in 1989 only 15 per cent said they had done so).[13]

Fragmentary though the evidence may be, there is no doubt that illegal drug use is widespread. In some areas and some social groups, it has become ingrained and to an extent socially accepted. Reviewing the epidemiology of illicit drug use, Plant concludes:

'The main point to emphasise is that a quarter to a third of people in Britain appear to have used some form of illegal drug, probably cannabis, by the time they reach their twenties.'[14]

When Is Illegal Drug Use Problematical?

Estimates of the extent of drug use in the UK are both discouraging and encouraging. Legislators may well feel dissatisfied with laws which are disregarded by as much as 30

---

12 Rt. Hon. John Patten, MP, Home Office News Release, 8 May 1991.

13 See Alun Michael, MP, *Cutting the Lifeline*, published by the Labour Party, May 1993.

14 M.A. Plant, 'The epidemiology of illicit drug-use and misuse in Britain', in Susanne MacGregor (ed.), *Drugs and British Society*, London: Routledge, 1989.

per cent of the young population, but some comfort can be found in the relatively small proportion who become dependent users.

No illegal drug use is free from risk. Even 'ecstasy', despite its benign image, has been held responsible for several deaths in the UK.[15] Nevertheless, most teenage drug use is financed out of pocket money rather than by crime and does not lead to drug dependency in the vast majority of cases.

Even seriously dependent users of heroin and cocaine are able to control their habit and live reasonably normal and productive lives without imposing major costs on the rest of society. The serious medical and social costs of drug abuse are to be found in the behaviour of those who lead chaotic lives or engage in criminality to finance their addiction. Broadly speaking, such users fall into one of two categories. Some cannot cope with drugs. These are no more representative of drug users than alcoholics are representative of drinkers. The other category of problem users consists of those whose difficulties stem mainly from the illegality of drugs. In the next chapter it is argued that a high proportion of the social costs and medical risks of drug use is attributable not so much to drugs as to drug law.

---

15 G. Pearson, J. Ditton, R. Newcombe, and M. Gilman, 'Everything starts with an "E"', *Druglink*, Vol.10-11, November/December 1991.

II. THE UNEASY CASE FOR PROHIBITION

Some illegal drugs are addictive; most can damage the health of users, and the use of drugs by some people inflicts costs on others. In these respects, illegal drugs are no different from alcohol and tobacco, and have much in common with activities such as reckless driving. All these substances and activities are part of the class of commodities which economists call 'demerit goods'.

It is often supposed that governments have an obligation to restrain the demand for demerit goods. This claim is based on a desire to protect citizens from the consequence of their own actions (paternalism) and the existence of external costs (market failure). It is, however, difficult, as Littlechild and Wiseman have shown, to construct a generally acceptable intellectual framework within which to defend even relatively minor restrictions on consumer choice such as those imposed by taxes on cigarettes.[1] It is still more difficult to sustain a case for the total prohibition of psychoactive substances.

Paternalism

The paternalistic or 'caring externality' argument features prominently in the case for the prohibition of drugs since drug users are believed to be incompetent in the judgement of their own best interests. A subtler variant holds that even competent adults might wish to be saved from the consequences of their own decisions. Drug addiction, it is alleged, is particularly tragic because, like suicide, it cuts off future options. An addicted user might regret the decision to use drugs and might wish to abstain, but could be physically or psychologically incapable of doing so.

These points may be valid in some cases but they do not constitute a case for prohibition, except perhaps in the case of children. In principle, there is no reason why an informed

---

1 S.C. Littlechild and J. Wiseman, 'The political economy of the restriction of choice', *Public Choice*, Vol.51, 1986, pp.161-72.

adult should be prevented from using mind-altering substances provided that no harm is caused to others. Where information is lacking, a case might be made for the state provision of drug education. But a more powerful objection to intervention on paternalistic grounds lies in the inability of the state to achieve its objectives.

There is no guarantee that measures designed to reduce the demand for demerit goods will protect those most at risk. Unemployed young people, with poor prospects and little to lose, are far less likely to be deterred by legal penalties than mature people with a stake in conventional society. Still worse, prohibition may encourage the more dangerous sorts of drug use and harm many of those who are most vulnerable. Furthermore, as explained later in this chapter (below, pp. 25-28), the paternalistic case for prohibition depends on a view of drugs and drug addiction which exaggerates the health risks and the difficulty of breaking a drug habit.

Market Failure

Official drug policy documents place emphasis on the external costs which spill over from users to the rest of society.[2] External costs are a feature of all demerit goods. It is not claimed they are particularly large in the case of illegal drugs. Nevertheless, external costs create a divergence between marginal private and social costs which prevents markets from achieving a (Pareto) efficient allocation of resources. Welfare gains might therefore be expected from government action which reduced the demand for demerit goods.

Familiarity with the concept of 'government failure' leads economists to regard this conventional argument for market intervention with caution. The mere existence of external costs is not sufficient justification for government action. Intervention is justified if, and only if, governments can improve the working of markets or perform market functions more efficiently. Governments can, and sometimes do, make matters worse.

---

2 Home Office, *Tackling Drug Misuse: A Summary of the Government's Strategy*, 3rd edition, London: HMSO, 1988.

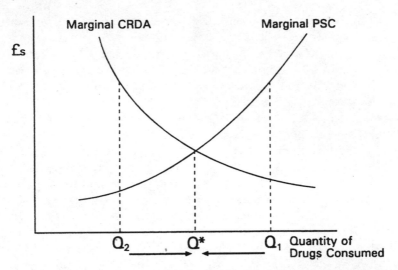

Figure 1: Marginal cost of reducing illegal drug use (CRDA) and the marginal private and social cost of illegal drug abuse (PSC) related to the quantity of drugs consumed, to give the optimum level of drug use at Q^*.

Furthermore, intervention of any sort is costly. The legal prohibition of drugs is exceptionally expensive to enforce. The costs of policy might therefore exceed its benefits. Economic efficiency principles require a policy to be pursued to the point where its marginal cost equals its marginal benefit; in practice it is most improbable that the prohibition of drugs is socially optimal.

Figure 1 (which takes no account of the perceived benefits of drugs to users) demonstrates why prohibition is likely to be non-optimal. The CRDA schedule shows the law enforcement cost of reducing drug use by one unit at each consumption level. The marginal cost of enforcement is likely to be low when consumption is high (detection is easy) but as drug use is reduced, it becomes increasingly expensive to track down an additional gramme.

The PSC function assumes it is possible to attach monetary values to all of the costs of drug abuse. It shows the hypothetical private and social costs imposed on society by the consumption of one extra unit of drugs. PSC is shown sloping up to the right to suggest that marginal costs might rise with consumption. Reading from right to left, the PSC

[24]

schedule can also be regarded as measuring the benefits (costs averted) of reducing drug use by one unit.

At any consumption level greater than Q^*, such as Q_1, the cost of drug abuse (PSC) exceeds the cost of law enforcement (CRDA) and society would benefit from stricter law enforcement. Conversely, at Q_2 and all consumption levels less than Q^*, the cost of law enforcement exceeds the cost of drug abuse, and a social saving could be achieved by relaxing law enforcement. Provided that the costs and benefits are regarded by society as Pareto comparable, and provided that the schedules intersect, it follows that an optimum level of drug use will be reached at Q^*. At this point the marginal cost of drug use equals the marginal cost of enforcement. Prohibition, however, aims to reduce drug use to zero (or close to it) and so cannot be socially optimal in the economist's sense.

Neither the paternalistic nor the market failure argument seems adequate to justify the prohibition of drugs for the reason given above. The remainder of this chapter deals with medical aspects of drug addiction and the high cost of prohibition. Both considerations detract still further from the case for prohibition.

The Dangers of Drug Use

It may be admitted that the case for prohibition is intellectually unattractive, but the immediate and under-standable reaction to the proposal that drugs should become legal is that psychoactive substances are too dangerous to be freely available. It is therefore surprising to a medical outsider to find no basis in science for distinctions between psychoactive drugs and other substances, which can be addictive and dangerous, but which are freely bought and sold.[3]

Even the most basic terms in the vocabulary of drug dependency such as 'dangerous substances', 'addiction' and 'drug abuse' are not susceptible to precise definition. Many innocuous substances, such as water, can be dangerous if used incorrectly, or in inappropriate quantities, and all drugs have side-effects. Drug addiction is associated with increased

---

3 Thomas S. Szasz, *Ceremonial Chemistry: The Ritual Persecutions of Drugs, Addicts and Pushers*, Garden City, New York: Doubleday, 1974.

tolerance to substances which change the behaviour of users in ways that create social or medical problems. But this is not a basis for distinctions between dependency on illegal drugs and many other strongly ingrained consumption habits.

The Royal College of Psychiatrists makes it plain that all drug use is risky.[4] Psychoactive substances have been associated with a wide range of medical and behavioural disorders, and some such drugs may be positively dangerous even in a single dose. By contrast, the consensus opinion from many investigations is that moderate cannabis use carries little, if any, health risk.

Even potent drugs such as heroin and other opiates can be taken for long periods without obvious ill-effects. Pharmaceutically pure heroin does not damage vital organs, and addicts have been maintained on stable doses for 40 years or more. Less is known about the long-term effects of cocaine and its derivative crack, but cocaine is not addictive in the same way as is heroin. Heavy cocaine users are prone to psychological and behavioural disorders which force them to abstain. It is rare for a person to be addicted for more than two or three years, although a Cheshire woman was maintained in good health on cocaine for 55 years.[5]

For some purposes, particularly the treatment of addicts, the pharmacological diversity of psychoactive drugs is important. Amphetamines and cocaine are stimulants; opiates and barbiturates are relaxants; and others such as LSD, cannabis, and ecstasy are hallucinogens or euphoriants. Most of these substances have not been subjected to clinical trials and a great deal remains unknown about their properties and long-term effects.

This uncertainty is by itself a powerful reason for exercising caution, but there is a sense in which pharmacology is irrelevant. Psychoactive drugs affect different people in different ways according to past experience, expectations and the social context within which they are used.[6] It is scarcely ever possible to predict the effect of drugs on an

---

4 Royal College of Psychiatrists, *Drug Scenes*, London: Gaskell, 1987.

5 R. Brown and R. Middlefell, 'Fifty-five years of cocaine dependence', *British Journal of Addiction*, Vol.84, 1989, p.946.

6 Norman E. Zinberg, *Drug, Set and Setting: The Basis for Controlled Intoxicant Use*, New Haven: Yale University Press, 1984.

individual user. Furthermore, some addicts are willing to substitute between drugs with quite different chemical properties, according to price and availability. This phenomenon suggests that users are not so much addicted to a particular chemically induced experience as to a way of life, or a means of ingestion – usually smoking or injecting.

The method of ingestion has a powerful influence on the risks of drug use. Inhaling the fumes of any drug, including cannabis, can cause lung damage, but intravenous injection is more dangerous. Injection is not inherently hazardous, but drug users who are inexpert and casual about hygiene are prone to overdosing and infection.

No one doubts the danger of drugs, but lurid reporting has created a misleading impression of the nature of drug abuse and has exaggerated its medical risks. The popular stereotype of an addict as a person who consumes increasingly large doses of heroin before dying of an overdose bears scarcely any relation to the known facts. Heroin addiction is a chronically relapsing condition which, on average, lasts for 10 to 15 years.[7] Some addicts respond to treatment, but most give up of their own volition, sometimes at a turning point in their lives such as marriage, the birth of a child or obtaining a job.

The health of female drug addicts is of special concern since most are of child-bearing age. Neither opiates nor cocaine are known to produce foetal abnormalities, but withdrawal during pregnancy carries a risk of premature labour and foetal distress. The babies of drug-dependent mothers are born addicted and need treatment for withdrawal symptoms. In most cases, however, addicted infants can be weaned from dependence in a matter of days, presumably because there is no psychological dimension to their addiction.[8]

Giving up drugs can be frightening and painful. Patients have described it as like a severe bout of influenza, but withdrawal symptoms subside in a matter of weeks and, in this respect, heroin is far less addictive than nicotine. Drug users proceed through frequent cycles of withdrawal and re-

---

7 G.V. Stimson and E. Oppenheimer, *Heroin Addiction*, London: Tavistock, 1982.

8 Institute for the Study of Drug Dependency, *Drugs, Pregnancy and Child Care*, London, 1990.

addiction (like tobacco users and weight-watchers). The problem is not so much giving up but rather of avoiding re-addiction.

For a minority of heavily dependent users the costs of drug abuse can be high and are found in reduced quality of life, morbidity and premature mortality. These costs spill over to friends and family and in costs to the health and social services. They are a matter of concern, but costs of this sort are common to all demerit goods. The vast majority of illegal drug users are not addicted in any medical sense. Most are not ill, and at least 95 per cent are not seeking to abstain at any one time.

The Costs of Anti-Drug Law

Prohibition creates a large stream of private costs to users and external costs to the rest of society. Viewed globally, the pursuit of illegal drug money, associated with gangsterism and political corruption, is the major external cost of drug law. Prohibition also imposes large enforcement and sentencing costs on the Exchequer and external costs on the private sector in the form of drug-related crime. Moreover, it adds considerably to the medical risks of drug use.

Law Enforcement Costs

Drug law enforcement costs, found mainly in police services and HM Customs and Excise, have never been satisfactorily disentangled. However, the average cost of employing a police officer in 1987-88 was £28,509 (total police budget divided by number of officers). On this basis, the 1,244 specialist police officers deployed in drug squads at the beginning of 1989 cost approximately £35 million.[9] To this should be added the budget of the National Drugs Intelligence Unit, which was £4·3 million in 1989-90,[10] and the cost of the Home Office Drugs Branch Inspectorate which is unknown.

---

9 *Hansard*, Written Answers, cols.1,065-66, 28 July 1989. (Answers to two questions from Mr Frank Dobson to Lord James Douglas-Hamilton and Mr Peter Lloyd.)

10 House of Commons Home Affairs Committee, Session 1988-89, Seventh Report, *Drug Trafficking and Related Serious Crime*, Vol.I, London: HMSO, 1989.

An extra 330 officers were needed to compensate for the extra work created by the Drug Trafficking Offences Act 1986.[11] Officers engaged in asset seizure are probably more expensive to employ than the average policeman, but taking an average figure, asset seizure probably costs a further £8·5 million a year. The assets seized are a source of revenue to the Exchequer but discussions on how these 'profits' might be used proved premature. In the first three years of operation, assets worth £8 million had been made subject to confiscation orders but significant shortfalls were reported between the amounts of the confiscation order and the amounts actually received.[12] 'Shortfalls' occur because it is difficult and expensive to trace and actually seize the assets.

In the financial year ending 31 March 1993, HM Customs and Excise's expenditure on drug law enforcement work is estimated at £120-150 million.[13] These figures, and those for police expenditure, relate only to the cost of specialist officers. They take no account of the considerable amount of drug work performed by other enforcement agents in the course of general duties. The government also makes grants to United Nations' agencies and foreign governments of £2-3 million annually, part of which is used to enforce drug law.

Sentencing Costs

The Exchequer bears the cost of prosecuting persons accused of drug law offences and also pays a high proportion of defence costs through the legal aid scheme. In 1988, 3,523 people were sentenced to immediate custody for drug offences. A calculation, which entails estimating the average length of a sentence (corrected for remission and probation) and the use of an average figure for the cost to the prison service, put the total cost of custodial sentences for drug offenders at approximately £49 million a year. In addition, account has to be taken of the cost of remand in custody, and minor sentences such as probation orders, community service orders and parole supervision. Estimates do not take account

---

11 *Ibid.*, Vol.II.

12 *Ibid.*

13 *HM Customs and Excise Annual Report*, Cm.2353, London: HMSO, October 1993.

of the greater-than-average costs of detaining drug users who create special problems for the prison service.

Drug-Related Crime

Not all crime committed by drug users can be attributed to the need to finance a drug habit, but strong evidence suggests that a high proportion of acquisitive crime is of this nature. In 1985 one-half of the convicted burglars in Wirral, Merseyside, were thought to be heroin users.[14] A study of heroin users attending the Liverpool Drug Dependency Unit reported that between 1985 and 1987, 90 per cent financed part of their habit from shoplifting or burglary. They spent, on average, £40 a day on drugs.[15]

Estimates of the value of goods stolen by drug users depend on evidence from small studies on the amount spent on drugs, and the proportion which is financed by crime. Wagstaff and Maynard settled for an estimate of total expenditure on heroin alone of between £111·7 and £237·8 million in 1984.[16] Taking the mid-point, and assuming that half of drug expenditure was financed by crime suggested that heroin users alone needed an illegal income of £87·4 million in 1984. Most drug users are unsophisticated thieves who steal clothes, leather goods and electrical equipment which have a low value in markets for stolen goods. If it is assumed that 'fences' pay one-fifth of market value, drug users would have needed to steal goods valued at £437 million. Wagstaff and Maynard's estimate was conservative. If allowance is made for other drugs, and the average drug dependent person steals goods worth only £20 a day, estimates of the order of £1,000 million seem reasonable for 1984.

A similar calculation, based on somewhat different assumptions, puts the value of drug-related theft in 1993 for

---

14 H. Parker, K. Bakx and R. Newcombe, 'The New Heroin Users: Prevalence and Characteristics in Wirral, Merseyside', *British Journal of Addiction*, Vol.82, 1987, pp.147-58.

15 C.S.J. Fazey, *The Evaluation of Liverpool Drug Dependency Clinic*, Report to the Mersey Regional Health Authority, 1987.

16 A. Wagstaff and A. Maynard, *Economic Aspects of the Illicit Drug Market and Drug Enforcement Policies in the United Kingdom*, Home Office Research Study No.95, London: HMSO, 1988.

England and Wales at £1,999 million. This is approximately 50 per cent of the total value of theft in 1993 and amounts to £114 per household.[17]

The cost of drug-related crime falls partly on the Exchequer and partly on the private sector. Police forces, the legal system and the prison service bear the cost of investigation, prosecution and sentencing. These costs must be large but cannot be identified from published data.

Most stolen goods are not lost to society but redistributed. If, however, the gains to thieves and the receivers of stolen goods are ignored, the cost to society of drug-related theft consists of the whole value of goods stolen, together with the pecuniary and social costs of avoiding theft. The cost of avoiding theft includes expenditure on alarm systems and other security devices. Other costs, no less real because they are hard to quantify, are the fear of theft and violence which make some people afraid to go out at night.

Drug Use in Illegal Markets

One of the few claims which is not controversial in this contentious field is that prohibition makes drug use a great deal more dangerous than it need be.[18] The high price of illegal drugs encourages injecting – the most economical method of ingestion. Injecting is said to give the most sensation per unit of cost, and none of the drug is lost to the atmosphere as with smoking. At high prices, users are more likely to share doses and needles, so the risk of transmitting disease is increased. If some drug users finance their habit from prostitution, infections can be communicated to the general public.

Other hazards stem from the difficulty of gauging the quality and potency of drugs in illegal markets. Street heroin may contain toxic substances or adulterants insoluble in water, which can cause ulceration and septicaemia. In 1994, people died in Bristol and in Glasgow from overdoses of heroin which was exceptionally pure by street standards. The risk of overdosing is also high after periods of imprisonment or voluntary abstinence, which reduce toleration to drugs.

---

17 *Drugs: The Need for Action*, A Labour Party Document, 11 February 1994.

18 John Ellard, 'The drug offensive', *Modern Medicine of Australia*, December 1989.

The likelihood that drug users will spend some time in prison adds further risks. The prison system is one route by which HIV infection passes to the non-drug using, heterosexual community. In 1990, official estimates put the number of 'serious drug users' in prisons at 1,800, but the National Association of Probation Officers believes the true figure to be between five and 10 times greater.[19] In England and Wales, 50-70 prisoners were recorded as being infected with HIV in 1991, but this was also thought to be an underestimate. The Prison Reform Trust suggested a figure of around 700.[20] This contention was supported by evidence from Bristol prison where the introduction of confidential counselling increased the number of inmates recorded as HIV+ from two to 24. A small study of ex-prisoners found that 66 per cent of convicted drug offenders continued to inject in gaol. More than half shared needles and 10 per cent had sex in gaol.[21]

Other public health risks occur to the extent that addicts do not seek medical attention. Injecting drug users are prone to hepatitis, but AIDS is of the greatest concern. Pregnant users, fearing that their children may be taken into care, are reluctant to declare their addiction and may not be treated optimally.

Close examination of the circumstances surrounding personal tragedies which have resulted from drug use would show that a high proportion are attributable to the risks of using drugs in illegal markets. Furthermore, far from correcting market failure, prohibition creates whole categories of external costs – social and economic. Prohibition appears flawed in principle, but there are still more compelling reasons to believe that it does not work in practice. They are discussed in Chapter III.

---

19 John Carvel, 'Drug use an added problem in jail, say probation officers', *The Guardian*, 9 April 1990.

20 Richard Smith, 'Failures of prison HIV policies', *British Medical Journal*, Vol.302, 16 February 1991.

21 *The Observer*, 29 July 1990.

III. THE FAILURE OF PROHIBITION

Since the introduction of prohibition in Britain in 1920, a tension has existed between the medical and penal approaches to drug addiction. The maintenance of registered drug users by National Health Service clinicians is an important aspect of policy (discussed in Chapter IV), so the medical view of drug dependency as an illness requiring treatment appears to have prevailed. But for the past 20 years, the main thrust of UK drug policy has been directed to the enforcement of drug law, aiming to eliminate illegal markets by making the use and exchange of drugs expensive and risky.

To this end, the UK and all signatories of the United Nations' Conventions on drugs are committed to policies directed at both the supply and the demand sides of the illegal drug market. Supply-side policy tries to reduce the amount of drugs which reaches the illegal market by imposing penalties on producers and distributors either within the UK or overseas. Demand-side policy attempts to reduce the demand for drugs by means which may be coercive (legal penalties for possession) or persuasive (education programmes).

Supply-Side Policy in Producer Countries

No clear distinction can be made between producer and consumer countries since addiction is growing rapidly in Third World producer countries, and Western countries produce a wide variety of drugs – both natural and synthetic. Nevertheless, public concern concentrates on heroin and cocaine, produced mainly in Asia and South America.

For 70 years, the international community, spurred by the USA, has used diplomacy and financial and military assistance to persuade producer countries to control drug production. Despite this effort, supply-side policies have made no discernible impact on the global availability of drugs. Drug law enforcement is hampered in producer countries by poor communications, inadequate funding and political instability. Where the drug trade is a major source of employment, income and foreign exchange, governments lack incentive to comply with international law.

Even if the will and the means exist to tackle illegal drug production in any particular country, international efforts tend to be minimal because of the highly competitive nature of the trade. There are many producers and many alternative routes between producer and consumer countries, so local success in restricting supply simply causes the trade to move across international borders. The virtual eradication of illegal opium production in Turkey in the late 1960s caused production to shift to Pakistan and South East Asia without major interruptions of supply to the market. Similarly, if US military action reduces the supply of cocaine from Colombia, the trade will pass to distributors of other nationalities who compete violently for market share.

The United Nations Fund for Drug Abuse Control (UNFDAC) has claimed local success in Turkey, Burma and Mexico for crop substitution schemes. It has also been suggested by President Alberto Fujimori that crop substitution could be made viable in Peru where institutional imperfections make coca production artificially profitable.[1] He argues that an oppressive bureaucracy and legal restraints on trade make transactions much more expensive in legal markets than in illegal markets. Furthermore, since legal costs prevent peasants from establishing property rights, they have incentive to grow coca, which requires relatively little attention, in preference to legal crops, such as coffee, which need more capital and more commitment to the land. Land reform, coupled with an assault on bureaucracy, which increased the profitability of legal crops relative to the profitability of coca, would improve the effectiveness of crop substitution programmes.

Imaginative proposals of this sort may have potentiality in some countries, but economists have thought that crop substitution schemes will be expensive.[2] This view has

---

1 Alberto Fujimori, *The Fujimori Initiative* ('A Policy for the Control of Drugs and Alternative Development'), Lima, Peru: Instituto Libertad y Democracia, 26 October 1990.

2 J. Holahan, 'The economics of the control of the illegal supply of heroin', *Public Finance Quarterly*, Vol.1, No.4, 1973, pp.467-77.

recently been supported in an official US administration document which concludes that 'crop substitution is not a promising strategy for reducing coca cultivation in the Andes'.[3] Crop substitution programmes will also be ineffective unless the acreage under cultivation can be controlled, which is difficult in an industry where the factors of production are abundant so that supply is highly elastic. In South America, 2,500,000 square miles of land are said to be capable of supporting coca production. The opium poppy can be cultivated over a still larger area. Labour is readily available at current wage rates, and the technology is simple.

Under these conditions, existing growers may accept the subsidy, but illegal drugs will continue to be grown on new land. Effective acreage control requires expensive, continuous surveillance by incorruptible administrators over terrain which is scarcely accessible even from the air. This is not within the capability of most Third World drug-producing countries. It is certain that the constructive and imaginative work conducted by UNFDAC cannot make a global impact on drug supplies without an injection of resources which exceeds by far the amounts governments are willing to commit at present.

Perhaps the most withering indictment of supply-side policy is found in the USA which is one of the world's largest producers of cannabis. It seems unreasonable to expect Third World countries to control drug production when the US government is incapable of achieving this end within its own territorial limits.

Domestic Supply-Side Policy

Domestic supply-side policies attempt to reduce the amount of drugs which reach the UK market by acting against dealers rather than users. Policies differ in their quantitative impact and their cost-effectiveness according to whether legal interventions are made at the point of entry into the country, or at the street level.[4] But all supply-side measures – seizures,

---

[3] R. Lee and P. Clawson, *Crop Substitution in the Andes*, Washington DC: Office of National Drug Control Policy, December 1993.

[4] Peter Reuter and Mark Kleiman, 'Risks and prices: an economic analysis of drug enforcement', in M. Tonry and N. Morris (eds.), *Crime and Justice: An Annual Review of Research*, Vol.7, 1986.

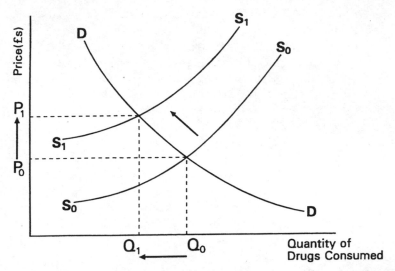

Figure 2: The effect of law enforcement on the supply-side of the market for an illegal drug of specified purity.

fines, imprisonment, confiscation of assets – act like a probabilistically incurred tax on dealers. Their effect is to increase the cost of doing business in the illegal market.

The impact of supply-side policy is shown in Figure 2, which represents the market for a particular drug of specified purity, at a point in time. Street price is measured vertically, and is related on the horizontal axis to the quantity of the drug which is bought and sold. The demand schedule, DD, shows the amount which users will buy at each price and is drawn with a negative slope to suggest that greater quantities will be purchased at lower prices.[5]

The supply schedule, initially at S_0, indicates the amounts of the drug which criminal firms will offer to the market at each price. There are no scarce factors of production for natural or synthetic drugs, so supply is probably elastic over a wide price range. The intersection of DD and S_0 establishes an equilibrium price at P_0, and an equilibrium quantity at Q_0.

Suppose that the government now intensifies law enforcement against dealers. More severe legal penalties, or

---

5 Demand curves for addictive substances do not slope upwards. A demand schedule is defined at a point in time for given tastes. Addiction is a process over time. This point was made by A.J. Culyer, 'Should social policy concern itself with drug abuse?', *Public Finance Quarterly*, Vol.1, No.4, 1973, pp.449-56.

an increased probability of getting caught, increases costs to dealers. This is represented in Figure 2 by a shift in the supply curve from S_0 to S_1. The effect is to increase price to P_1 and reduce the quantity consumed to Q_1.[6] The next sub-section considers the relative size of the price and quantity effects and their impact on the income of drug users.

(a) Price Effect

Experience leaves no doubt that supply-side policy has a powerful effect on price. Prices and purity in the illegal market vary considerably, but for some years £80 has been a typical price for 1 gramme of heroin of no more than .40 per cent purity. If it was available on the illicit market, 1 gramme of 100 per cent purity would sell for about £200.

Opium derivatives are used in the treatment of pain and coughs and in anti-diarrhoeal preparations. At prices prevailing in November 1993, the cost to the NHS of 2 grammes of diamorphine BP (heroin, 100 per cent pure) was £10·71, plus a dispensing fee estimated at £1.[7] Heroin therefore costs the NHS £5·86 per gramme which is about 3 per cent of the price on the illegal market.

Pharmaceutical heroin is still cheaper in some of its preparations, and the NHS buys from a monopolist supplier which had 87 per cent of the market in 1987, and was the subject of a Monopolies Commission Report in 1989.[8] Some studies claim that the street prices of expensive drugs such as heroin and cocaine are 60-100 times higher than legal pharmaceutical prices.[9]

---

6 This conventional price-adjustment model may seem inappropriate to some drug markets where dealers respond to shortages by adulterating the drug, rather than by increasing its price. In a quality-adjustment model, supply-side policy reduces the potency of drugs rather than the quantity consumed. This mechanism works only so long as drug users fail to detect the decline in purity. When users 'cotton-on', they buy larger quantities. In this way, the quality-adjustment model produces predictions similar to the price-adjustment model, but by different processes.

7 *National Health Service Drug Tariff*, London: HMSO, November 1993.

8 Monopolies and Mergers Commission, *Opium Derivatives*, Cm.630, London: HMSO, April 1989.

9 Robert J. Michaels, 'The market for heroin before and after legalisation', in Ronald Hamowy (ed.), *Dealing with Drugs*, Lexington, Mass.: D.C. Heath and Company, 1987, pp.289-326.

(b) Quantity Effect

Supply-side policy definitely increases drug prices, but the impact on consumption depends on the price elasticity of demand. If the demand for drugs is elastic, a small increase in price will induce a proportionately large reduction in quantity demanded, and supply-side policies will be effective. If demand is inelastic, law enforcement will be less effective.

The scarcity and poor quality of data on clandestine drug markets has left economists free to speculate on the likely value of the price elasticity of demand in a literature surveyed by Wagstaff and Maynard.[10] Intuition suggests that the demand for addictive substances must be inelastic, or what other meaning can be attached to the notion of drug dependency? However, demand is not *perfectly* inelastic, and it could be elastic for some users at fairly low prices and for all users at very high prices.

Blair and Vogel proposed that demand is likely to be price inelastic for addicts, but much more elastic for occasional users.[11] This hypothesis is depicted in Figure 3 where the demand function is ABC. Intensified law enforcement, which shifts S_0 to S_1, will be effective in reducing drug consumption in the range BC by deterring occasional users. At some quantity Q* and price P*, only seriously dependent users remain in the market, and further supply-side measures will be ineffective.

It has also been argued that if law enforcement is pursued with sufficient vigour, a price must be reached at which demand is elastic even for addicts.[12] At this high price, addicts would not be able to steal enough to support their habits, or they would simply reach a point where the cost of a drug habit exceeded its benefits. While this is acceptable as a theoretical possibility, the costs of enforcing the law so stringently would be very large.

It cannot be denied that demand may be elastic in some circumstances, so it is not possible to say that supply-side

10 Wagstaff and Maynard, *op. cit.*

11 R.D. Blair and R.J. Vogel, 'An economic analysis of the illicit drug market', *Public Finance Quarterly*, Vol.1, No.4, 1973, pp.457-67.

12 M.D. White and W.A. Luksetich, 'Heroin: price elasticity and enforcement strategies', *Economic Inquiry*, Vol.21, 1983, pp.557-64.

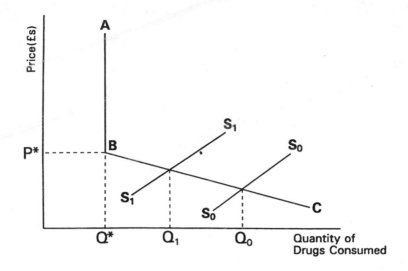

Figure 3: Supply-side policy effective until price P* is reached, when casual users have been deterred and only addicts remain in the market.

policies will always perform badly, but a final consideration makes this most likely. All of the literature concerns the demand for a single drug, heroin. The demand for any single drug is bound to be somewhat elastic since, to a greater or lesser extent, all drugs are substitutes one for another. There are, however, far fewer substitutes for all psychoactive substances than for any individual substance, so the demand for all drugs is bound to be inelastic and especially so for seriously dependent users. It follows that supply-side policy will have a larger effect on prices than on the quantity of drugs consumed.

(c) Income Effect

If the demand for drugs is price inelastic, supply-side policy does not merely fail – it increases the total expenditure on drugs and adds to the social cost of illegal drug use. This is illustrated most clearly in the extreme case shown in Figure 4, where demand is perfectly inelastic. If law enforcement is intensified, the supply curve shifts to S_1 and price increases to P_1, but there is no change in the quantity demanded.

In initial equilibrium, total expenditure is represented by the area P_0Q_0 in Figure 4. At the new equilibrium, users will

[39]

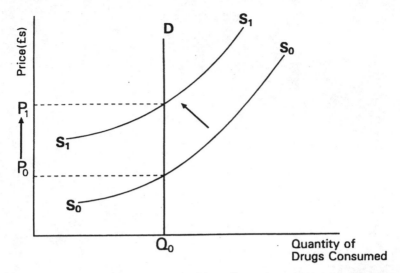

Figure 4: The effect of supply-side policy when demand for a drug is perfectly inelastic.

need a larger income, shown by the area P_1Q_0, to maintain their habits. To the extent that some drug users will find the extra income in theft and prostitution, the costs of illegal drug use spill over to the rest of society.

Over time, supply-side policies may actually increase the demand for drugs. Some users will respond to higher prices by dealing. Users have an incentive to sell to friends, drug use becomes contagious, and the demand curve in Figure 4 will shift to the right. This is one of the paradoxes of prohibition. Law enforcement encourages some drug use, and if demand is perfectly (or only fairly) inelastic, supply-side policy increases the external costs of drug abuse.

Demand-Side Policy

The general effect of demand-side policy is shown in Figure 5. A reduction in demand from D_0 to D_1 brings about a fall in the quantity demanded from Q_0 to Q_1, and a fall in street price from P_0 to P_1. Since the supply is thought to be elastic, demand-side policy is likely to be highly effective in reducing drug use. This result can be achieved either by intensified law enforcement against users (rather than dealers) or through drug education programmes.

[40]

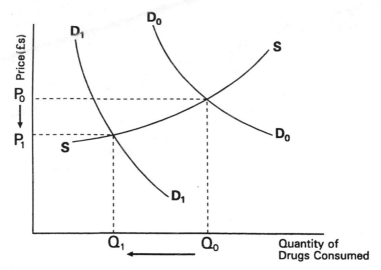

Figure 5:   Reducing illegal drug use through demand-side policies.

Law enforcement against users works by increasing the full cost of drug habits. The full cost is made up of the street price plus transaction costs. Transaction costs include the cost in time (and perhaps danger) of seeking out a supplier, and the risk of being caught in possession. Tougher penalties and tighter enforcement increase these costs and tend to reduce demand.

Stern action against young offenders may have salutary effects, but coercive demand-side policies are unattractive. They pass problems to the courts and the prison system both of which are over-stretched and ill-equipped to deal with them. More attractive are drug education programmes which inform, persuade and frighten potential and existing users in the direction of abstinence.

Good efforts are made in this area by statutory and voluntary agencies, but drug education programmes are in their infancy and it is difficult to demonstrate their effectiveness. Professional drug workers were severely critical of the government's mass media advertising campaign in the mid-1980s which excited curiosity about heroin in parts of the country where it was previously unknown. The same problem has been encountered with the drug cyclizine, which is the active ingredient in a readily available pharmaceutical product. In a highly localised part of

England, cyclizine is injected in a particularly dangerous manner. The problem for drug workers is how to warn against these dangers without advertising the product.[13]

People in positions of authority encounter another pitfall by making blanket condemnations of drugs which users know to be untrue. A ministerial statement, widely quoted in 1989, claimed that crack is 'addictive instantly, and addiction to it is incurable'. This statement was known by drug users to be incorrect since many people had already tried crack and were not in any sense addicted. Similarly, several official statements have claimed that drug use, in addition to many other things, leads to poverty. For many it does, but in Manchester and elsewhere, it is alleged that some teenage dealers earn more than their teachers.

The tendency to exaggerate the dangers of drug use is a recurring feature in the history of drug policy and a source of embarrassment to professional drug workers whose clients know more about drugs than most politicians. The danger is that statements by public figures which are less than accurate tend to undermine the solemnity of their message.

It is difficult to show that drug education has made any impact so far. Demand reduction by education may be the best hope for the future, but the techniques are undeveloped and evidence from campaigns against alcohol and tobacco suggests that speedy results cannot be expected.

The Time-Horizon

It has been argued that anti-drug policies are unlikely to achieve their objectives. As Sam Peltzman has observed, law enforcement in the UK seems to have been highly effective in seizing increasingly large amounts of drugs. Yet these policies, which tend to increase street prices, have been more than offset by increased criminal productivity, so that in real terms prices have remained constant, or have actually fallen during some periods.[14] Supply-side policies are fundamentally flawed since as long as drug profits are sufficiently high, some people will risk any legal penalty for trafficking. If

---

13 G. Pearson, M. Gilman and P. Traynor, 'The Limits of Intervention', *Druglink*, May/June 1990, pp.12-13.

14 Sam Peltzman, 'The Failure of Enforcement', *British Journal of Addiction*, Vol.84, 1989, pp.469-70.

governments wish to fight market forces, the demand-side approach is superior but slow and uncertain in its effectiveness.

Not everyone will be convinced by these arguments. Some will claim that the war on drugs has scarcely started, and a massive increase in law enforcement expenditure could save current policy from total discredit. However, no one is prepared to argue that the drug war will be won quickly.

Policies take effect over time and whether the benefits which are claimed for them accrue over six months, 10 years, or two generations is a matter of the greatest importance. The time-horizon is particularly important in drug policy since drug abuse is contagious, and concern is expressed for children and unborn generations. It is therefore possible that alternatives to current policy such as legalisation, which some regard as worse than second best, could be preferable to more generally acceptable policies which are slow to take effect.

IV. ALTERNATIVES TO THE DRUG WAR

This chapter considers alternatives to current drug policy which fall short of full legalisation. Most envisage relaxation of the law as it applies to possession only. The term 'decriminalisation' is often used to describe policies of this sort. Legalisation goes further. It would abolish legal penalties for dealing as well for possession.

Distinctions Between Substances

In view of the large number of psychoactive substances which exist and uncertainties about their properties, it is difficult to sustain distinctions between 'hard' and 'soft' drugs. Even so, some of the less powerful sorts could be treated differently under the law from heroin and cocaine. Decriminalising cannabis would reduce its relative price and, other things equal, the consumption of cannabis relative to other drugs would increase. This would be a welcome corrective to the tendency in illegal markets for dangerous drugs to drive out the safer sorts.

In a similar vein, Anthony Henman has argued that coca leaves are classed quite improperly in the United Nations' Conventions with much more potent substances.[1] HRH The Princess Royal has vouched for the properties of coca tea, which she tried in Bolivia.[2] A similar experiment in the UK could attract a fine and a prison sentence. Henman has suggested that peasant producers would benefit from the legalisation of coca and that coca leaves could be marketed in the West as a substitute for other drugs. Coca may also have therapeutic potential as a slow-acting substitute for more dangerous stimulants such as amphetamines.

---

1 Anthony Henman, 'Coca: an alternative to cocaine?', in Arnold S. Trebach and Kevin B. Zeese (eds.), *Drug Policy 1989-1990: A Reformer's Catalogue*, Washington DC: The Drug Policy Foundation, 1989.

2 'Princess attacks "crime" of drug abuse', *The Daily Telegraph*, 11 April 1990.

As a partial approach to some drug problems, the de-criminalisation of cannabis and coca seems a fairly riskless first step. The principal fear is that criminal firms would react by concentrating their marketing strategies on more profitable drugs. This tendency was noted in the USA in the 1970s, where cannabis was decriminalised in some states and dealers switched to heroin and cocaine trafficking.

Distinctions Between Users and Dealers

The popular notion that drug dealers are wicked, whereas users are merely weak, is a basis for distinctions in law between possession and trafficking. As is well known, this distinction is not clear-cut. Some users act as suppliers for a circle of friends, do not make profits, and would be offended by the suggestion that they are dealers. Others deal mainly or wholly as a means of financing their habits, and have much more in common with the victims of drug abuse than with wealthy traffickers.[3]

It is doubtful whether the public interest is served by committing drug users and small dealers to prison where rehabilitation is scarcely possible. Drug users add to the problems of the prison service, and the view that most offenders would be better directed to medical care, rather than to prison, is now widely accepted.

Harm Reduction Policy

Harm reduction policy (HRP) is the most important recent development in drug policy. HRP tackles public health issues directly by seeking to reduce the personal and social costs of drug use. The principal ingredients of most programmes are educational and advisory services, syringe exchanges, and treatment and maintenance services. Some programmes also employ outreach workers to contact those at risk from HIV infection and other diseases – mostly prostitutes.

Demand reduction is one aim of HRP, but abstinence is not regarded as a realistic short-term goal for most dependent users. Policy therefore proceeds in a pragmatic fashion through a hierarchy of more achievable objectives.

---

[3] Nicholas Dorn and Nigel South, 'Drug markets and law enforcement', *British Journal of Criminology*, Vol.30, 1990, pp.171-87.

Non-users are urged to abstain. Users are advised to reduce doses and to avoid the most potent drugs and the riskier means of ingestion. Users who insist on injecting are offered advice on safe techniques. Needle sharing is strongly discouraged but those who persist are taught to clean equipment, and urged to reduce the number of people with whom equipment is shared.[4]

Before the discovery of AIDS, governments were reluctant to sanction harm-reduction policies which might seem to condone drug use and require police co-operation. Police co-operation is essential because if the law were strictly enforced, clients could be arrested in the vicinity of a clinic for the possession of any trace of a prohibited substance. The realisation that AIDS poses a greater threat to public health than drug addiction removed political objections and most districts now provide services for drug users, although the range and quality is very uneven. In 1992 there were 272 needle exchange schemes in the UK. Several hundred pharmacies sell syringes and others distribute syringes provided free of charge by some health authorities.

HRP is radical in its departure from the strict prohibitionist position which takes abstinence as its principal objective. As public health services reach out to unregistered (criminal) drug users, the interests of public health have begun to prevail over the law. Pursued to its logical conclusion, harm-reduction edges the law in the direction of decriminalisation and legalisation.

The Dutch System

Dutch drug law is not much different from the British but the trend to decriminalisation is more advanced. Users are seldom charged for the possession of drugs of any sort. Heavy users are maintained on methadone, and harm-reduction services are better co-ordinated and more extensive than they are in the UK.[5] It is estimated that there are 15-20,000 drug

---

4 Russell Newcombe, 'The reduction of drug-related harm: a conceptual framework for theory, practice and research', in P.A. O'Hare, R. Newcombe, A. Matthews, E.C. Buning and E. Drucker (eds.), *The Reduction of Drug-Related Harm*, London: Routledge, 1992.

5 F. Ruter, *The Pragmatic Dutch Approach to Drug Control: Does It Work?*, Washington DC: Drug Policy Foundation, 1988.

addicts in Holland, most of them known to the authorities and receiving treatment.[6] Most drugs are readily available in Holland but at 0.14 per cent of the population, the prevalence rate is lower than in the UK (0.20 per cent), Germany (0.19 per cent), Denmark (0.20 per cent) and Italy (0.45 per cent).

Despite the ready availability of cheap, high-quality heroin, addiction rates have not increased in recent years. The average age of known heroin addicts rose from 27 years in 1981 to 30 years in 1987, and the proportion aged under 21 fell from 14 per cent to 5 per cent. The sale of cannabis remains illegal but has been tolerated in 'hash coffee shops' since 1980. There are about 300 in Amsterdam alone, but cannabis use has not increased and, compared with neighbouring countries, the number of users per head of population is thought to be low.[7]

The Dutch government spends relatively far less than the UK government on law enforcement and more on services to drug users. The decriminalisation of possession removes large numbers of offenders from the courts, and sparing use of prison sentences involves particularly high-cost savings. Drug-related crime is minimal and in general terms, the social and economic cost of drug abuse seems much lower in Holland than it is in the UK.

A Return to the 'British System'?

International law allows exceptions for the medical use of prohibited substances and leaves nation states free to decide which medical uses are legitimate. The 'British System' evolved from the report of the Rolleston Committee in 1926 which recommended that registered drug users judged unlikely or unready to abstain should receive drugs under medical supervision on prescription.[8] This system seemed to

---

6 E. Englesman, 'Dutch policy on the management of drug-related problems', *British Journal of Addiction*, Vol.84, 1989, pp.211-18.

7 Adriann C.M. Jansen, *Cannabis in Amsterdam: a geography of hashish and marijuana*, Muiderberg, The Netherlands: Editions Coutinho B.V., 1991.

8 *Departmental Committee on Morphine and Heroin Addiction* (Rolleston Committee), Ministry of Health, London: HMSO, 1926.

serve well for more than 40 years and has been widely praised as a humane approach to drug problems.[9]

Controlled availability of drugs to dependent users also appeals to economists as a reverse form of price discrimination which makes use of the difference between habitual and casual users in their demand elasticities.[10] A price discriminating criminal drug dealer would maximise profits by charging addicts, whose demand is inelastic, a higher price than casual users, whose demand is likely to be more sensitive to price. Controlled availability makes drugs freely available to addicts, but legal sanctions and high prices in illegal markets remain as a deterrent to new or casual users. In this way, seriously drug-dependent people, who generate most of the external costs of drug abuse, no longer have to commit crime. Under medical supervision their health is maintained, and many are able to hold jobs and live reasonably normal lives.

The National Health Service continues to operate a system of controlled availability, but it changed radically in response to increased heroin addiction in the 1960s.[11] The authority to prescribe heroin and cocaine was restricted to about 500 clinicians (mostly hospital-based psychiatrists) and drug therapy was centralised into Drug Dependency Units (DDUs). In the 1970s clinicians became reluctant to prescribe heroin, and switched from long-term to short-term maintenance therapy linked to the willingness of users to participate in treatment programmes. Almost all receive oral methadone, an opiate substitute as addictive as heroin but with effects which are longer lasting but less intense.

Drug Therapy

Clinicians resist long-term maintenance on the grounds that it is not a treatment, but drug therapy is one of the few areas in medicine which does not seem to have advanced in modern times. Relapse rates from treatment are high,

9 E. Schur, *Narcotic Addiction in Britain and America. The Impact of Public Policy*, London: Tavistock, 1963.

10 M.H. Moore, 'Policies to achieve discrimination on the effective price of heroin', *American Economic Review*, Vol.63, 1973, pp.270-77.

11 Virginia Berridge, 'Historical Issues', in Susanne MacGregor (ed.), *op. cit.*, pp.20-35.

perhaps 75 per cent, and this figure has not changed for at least 75 years.[12] It was hoped that DDUs would reduce the prevalence of drug addiction, but the terms and conditions on which treatment is offered act like a price which discourages many users. In particular, oral methadone is unattractive to many who inject. Drug users in medical treatment of any sort are less likely to commit crime and lead more organised lives than others, but large numbers of seriously drug dependent people do not present themselves for treatment.[13] For every registered user, there are between five and 10 others who prefer the high price and the hazards of the illegal market to the treatment offered by the NHS. The presumption must be that for most users the costs ('hassle' plus waiting time) must exceed the expected benefits (oral methadone plus the possibility of rehabilitation).

A few clinicians continue to prescribe opiates. In parts of the Mersey Health Region, for example, a small number of clients has received heroin, methadone, amphetamine or cocaine in injectable and smokeable forms.[14] This so-called experiment is much closer in spirit to the old 'British System' than the treatment pattern which prevails elsewhere and, unlike many drug therapies, it has been evaluated.[15] A sample of seriously drug dependent people was maintained in reasonably good health. Some patients were able to remain in work and the level of criminal activity was reduced. No prescribed drugs were shown to have leaked to the illegal market, and in one district (Widnes) it was said that the black market had ceased to exist.

Still more significantly, Liverpool has a large population of injecting drug users and is a port served by perhaps 1,000 prostitutes. In these conditions, a high incidence of HIV infection might have been expected. In fact, among injecting

12 Roderick E. McGrew, *Encyclopedia of Medical History*, London: Macmillan, 1985, p.98.

13 Joy Mott, 'Reducing heroin related crime', *Research Bulletin*, No.26, London: Home Office Research and Planning Unit, 1989, pp.30-33.

14 See 'RX Drugs', transcript of programme on *60 Minutes*, published in *CBS News*, Vol.XXV, No.15, 27 December 1992, pp.20-28.

15 C.S.J. Fazey, *op. cit.*

users it is probably less than 1 per cent, and many of the known cases did not acquire the infection locally. No other community can claim to have controlled HIV infection so well. No doubt many factors were at work, but well-co-ordinated drug services, police co-operation, and the willingness of several generations of clinicians to prescribe opiates (and thereby attract into treatment a high proportion of users most at risk) must have played a part.

At any point in time, most drug users do not wish to abstain. A drug user may, in the opinion of others, have problems but may not wish to confront them and may not be ill. This raises difficulties for clinicians whose principal responsibility is to treat sick people. Quite reasonably, a clinician may take the view that to maintain a user is not a form of treatment and that it is medically indefensible to give heroin to a drug addict.

On the other hand, drug dependency does not respond well to treatment of any sort, and a clinician could regard it as a duty to maintain a user in good health until he is ready to abstain. This very broad view of clinical responsibility has been expressed by Dr John Marks who has suggested that a doctor

> 'may well consider prescribing a tot of best Scotch whisky to an alcoholic, if it would stop his patient robbing someone and paying a gangster for adulterated meths'.[16]

As Marks implies, the decision to prescribe or not to prescribe bears on major social issues which reach far beyond the intimacy of the patient-doctor relationship.

Certainly, medical treatment which attracts so few users cannot be regarded as successful. A greater willingness to prescribe the drugs to which users are addicted, on terms and conditions reduced to the minimum that the medical profession can tolerate, offers the most constructive supply-side approach available in the present state of the law. However, the balance of medical opinion is strongly opposed to any such policy change. In these circumstances, it might be fruitful to inquire whether the availability of drugs is too

---

16 John Marks, 'The opiate prescribing debate continued', *British Journal of Psychiatry*, Vol.155, October 1989, p.566.

important to be left entirely to the discretion of the medical profession.

The Inevitability of Gradualism?

UK drug policy has softened in response to the AIDS threat and to the growing recognition of the inadequacy of the penal system as a means of dealing with drug problems. Recent reductions in prison sentences and the growth of harm-reduction policies are moving UK policy in the direction of the Dutch system.

In subsequent chapters, bold claims will be made for the social benefits of outright legalisation but it is open to critics to argue that no such dramatic change in the law is necessary, and that a more gradual approach is better suited to British conditions. Certainly it is sensible to inquire whether some of the benefits which will be claimed for legalisation might be acquired more cheaply and with less risk by alternative means. All of the options considered in this chapter have advantages over prohibition, but most represent easements of policy as it applies to users rather than dealers. Decriminalisation is only a partial approach. It does not tackle the illegal trade which prospers from an increase in drug use and sponsors terrorism and political corruption. Legalisation deals directly with the fundamental problem which is to wrest control of drug markets from criminals.

V. THE CASE FOR LEGALISATION

The case for legalisation stems from the contention that prohibition is wrong in principle (Chapter II) and does not work in practice (Chapter III). The argument proceeds to consider alternatives other than legalisation and concludes that, while many have merit, none strikes at the criminal control of drug markets which is responsible for a high proportion of the evils of drug abuse (Chapter IV). In this chapter, legalisation is proposed as a response to drug problems which offers substantial social savings and deals directly and swiftly with criminality.

For many years, debating drug issues was as much fun as playing tennis by oneself. Legalisation used to be dismissed as 'irresponsible' or 'unthinkable', but in recent years a growing number of people in authority, including senior ministers, have come to agree that there is a case to be answered and have responded with reasoned arguments.[1,2] Some of these objections are considered in a final section of this chapter.

The Benefits of Legalisation

The specific benefits of legalisation include cost savings to the Exchequer and the private sector; medical and social benefits to drug users and their families; reductions in public health risks; and less wear and tear on political and legal institutions. They are described briefly below.

1. Savings to the Exchequer

If the sale and use of psychoactive substances became legal, some part of the resources currently devoted to the enforcement of the drug laws would become available for other uses. Assuming that sales to children remained illegal, some drug

---

1 Rt. Hon. Douglas Hurd, MP, 'Drugs: Legalisation is no answer', Speech to the Derby North Conservative Association, 8 September 1989.

2 Council of Europe Social, Health and Family Affairs Committee, *Report on drug misuse and illicit trafficking and the question of legalisation*, Rapporteur Mr Rathbone, Strasbourg, 23 May 1990.

law enforcement expenditure would still be necessary, but large savings would be expected in police departments, HM Customs and Excise, and the legal and penal systems.

2. Drug-Related Crime

In competitive markets, legalisation would reduce the price of drugs dramatically; thus the cost of an average drug habit might not exceed the cost of an average cigarette habit. Some drug users would continue to steal, and some thieves would still use drugs, but many drug users would no longer need to commit crime to finance a drug habit. In consequence, drug-related acquisitive crime, the largest external cost category, should be greatly reduced.

3. Drug Users and Their Families

Habitual users would benefit in several ways. The fall in drug prices would be equivalent to a large increase in real income, most of which would become available for non-drug expenditure such as better food and shelter. Users would be released from the double jeopardy of having to finance an illegal habit by illegal means, and would be less exposed to criminal influences.

4. Medical Benefits

Legalisation offers medical benefits to drug users and non-users, and advantages to the medical profession. Some addicts would continue to lead chaotic lives and would remain impervious to advice, but cheap legal drugs would remove part of the incentive to the more dangerous sorts of drug use and remove the pressures which force users into prostitution. Drug users should be better integrated into society, more likely to be employed, and more amenable to treatment and advice. All of these tendencies would improve the health of drug users, but perhaps the most certain medical benefits would accrue from the replacement of adulterated street drugs by pharmaceutically pure products.

Non-users would benefit from a reduction in the risk of hepatitis and HIV infection and less drug-related illness would go untreated. Some people would also benefit medically from legalisation in a very direct way. Most illegal drugs have known medical uses.[3] Cannabis, for instance, is valuable in the treatment of glaucoma, probably the commonest disease of the eye, but cannabis cannot be prescribed without Home Office permission, which is seldom granted. More generally, legalisation would remove an inhibition to pharmacological research on illegal substances, and increase the possibility that other medical uses will be found for this class of drugs.

Finally, the medical profession would derive benefits from legalisation. The present situation cannot be satisfactory to clinicians. Treatment and rehabilitation facilities are clogged by users whose motivation to give up drug taking is weak or non-existent. Where addicts depend on doctors for drug supplies, consultations are reduced to bargaining rounds. Users try to disguise their reliance on street drugs to supplement the state ration by faking urine tests. Clinicians, acting in what they regard as the best interests of clients, are subjected to verbal abuse and even physical violence.

In the present situation, the treatment of drug dependency is frequently unrewarding and potentially dangerous. If drugs were legal, doctors would no longer be regarded as agents of the state; confidentiality and trust would be restored to the doctor-patient relationship; and doctors would be free to consult the best interests of their patients without legal constraints.

5. Social Control

All legal systems for the production and distribution of drugs allow the authorities to regain some measure of control over drug markets. In illegal markets most of the decisions concerning the types of products and their availability are made by criminals. In legal markets such decisions would be taken by law-abiding, tax-paying businessmen within a framework of law, and governments could tax and regulate the trade.

6. Legal and Political Institutions

For many, and especially those with Latin American experience, the principal merit of legalisation is that it would

---

3 Lester Grinspoon and James B. Bakalar, 'Medical uses of illicit drugs', in Hamowy, *op. cit.*

retard the spread of corruption and criminality which threatens the political and legal fabric of whole societies.

The threat of corruption is inherent in prohibition. In an illegal drug transaction there is no victim to complain of a breach in the law, as there usually is in crimes against persons and property. In that sense, drug offences are victimless. Strict drug law enforcement requires officers to operate under cover. They need to gain the confidence of criminals and may even commit crimes. In these situations policemen run a grave risk of becoming compromised.

When criminal firms are large and rich, bribery and corruption are not restricted to policemen and border guards. Already some illegal drug firms command more resources than some governments. For instance, the Medellin Cartel once offered to pay off the Colombian national debt. Drug profits are used to protect and expand markets, and to finance other sorts of criminality. In several countries, drug dealers have corrupted whole political and legal systems and present a serious threat to the authority of elected governments. Drug legalisation would deprive criminals of billions of pounds in profits annually.

Closer to home, it must be a matter for concern that perhaps one-third of young people have used an illegal drug. When the law is used to enforce the unenforceable, there is a fear that respect for the law and its agents will be weakened. Perhaps of equal concern is the way in which the peril of drug addiction has been exaggerated to justify incursions into civil liberties. This point has been made with special force in the United States where in drug cases standards of evidence have been lowered, powers of search and seizure have been expanded, and the presumption of innocence has been abrogated.

In the UK, Enoch Powell drew attention to the provisions of the Drug Trafficking Act 1986, which similarly breach one of the most fundamental principles of natural law by reversing the onus of proof from the accuser to the accused. The property of convicted drug offenders can be confiscated unless the defendant can prove that it was purchased with legally acquired funds.[4] Mr Powell's fear was that once a

---

4 J. Enoch Powell, *The Drug Trafficking Act versus Natural Justice*, London: Libertarian Alliance, 1987.

principle has been breached, the breach will almost certainly be widened. His prediction was rapidly confirmed in the Criminal Justice Act 1988 which applied the same principle to other serious crimes which result in proceeds in excess of £10,000.

Some Objections

Objections to legalisation are frequently put in the form of a series of questions. Those which concern issues of operational feasibility are discussed in Chapter VI. Others are considered below.

1. Would Legalisation Lead to an Epidemic of Drug Abuse?

Ending prohibition would make drugs cheap, pure and legal: drug use might therefore increase. It does not follow, however, that the consumption of all types of drugs would increase, or that drug-related harm would be greater than at present. Indeed, there are good reasons to suppose that harm would be reduced.

Nothing in the epidemiological literature suggests that any of the currently illegal drugs, except possibly cannabis, would ever approach alcohol and tobacco in popularity. Health concerns are a major influence on consumer behaviour. Smoking is in decline, and those who persist are likely to smoke tipped, low-tar cigarettes. The rising demand for decaffeinated tea and coffee, poly-unsaturated fats and organically grown foods are aspects of a wholly sensible approach to diet and drugs which is incompatible with the notion that large numbers of people only await legalisation before injecting heroin or cocaine into their veins.

If drugs were legal, more people might experiment, but addiction and other health problems need not increase. In a legal system, users would be more likely to avoid the most dangerous substances and the most dangerous forms of ingestion. The extent of the harm which drugs cause depends on the social circumstances in which they are used. In illegal markets, problematic drug use is strongly associated with poverty, unemployment, ill-health and crime. Legalisation would break, or at least modify, this association. Drug problems would still be a cause for concern, but not necessarily for alarm. Voluntary organisations and governments have power to moderate the danger of drug use, and private firms have incentives to seek safer substitutes for existing drugs.

Finally, not all the forces released by legalisation tend in the direction of increased consumption. To the extent that illegal drug use is an expression of rebellion by the young against parents and teachers, one element in the demand for drugs is removed. Drug use would become less exciting and even boring. Legalisation also removes the financial incentive for users to make recruits which is one cause of the growth of drug use in illegal markets.

2. Is Legalisation Morally Defensible?

Is it morally defensible to make substances freely available which will harm at least some people? This is a legitimate question, but proponents of legalisation do not concede the moral high ground to prohibitionists. Most of the atrocities committed in the pursuit of illegal drug money are attributable to prohibition. Prohibition causes the cost of drug abuse to spill over to millions in drug-related crime and public health risks, and prohibition harms many people by making drug use more dangerous than it need be. But there is a further fundamental immorality inherent in prohibition. Drug laws define people with problems as criminals. Drug law enforcement puts up drug prices and forces addicts into further criminality to finance their habits. A final twist to the inhumanity of prohibition is the failure to provide adequate social and medical facilities for those users who wish to abstain.

It is also suggested that legalisation is objectionable because it means giving in to criminals. Perhaps the politicians who make this point have in mind the embarrassment of admitting that the law has taken an untenable position. The truth is that the criminal drug trade owes its existence to anti-drug law and the most efficient way of dealing with criminals would be to remove the source of their excess profits by opening the trade to competition from legal firms.

3. Would Legalisation Seem to Condone Drug Use?

Politicians have asked how it is possible to reconcile serious warnings about the dangers of drug use with legalisation which might seem to condone it.[5] Their point is weakened when one realises that 30 per cent of young people do not take the warnings seriously. In any case, there should be no presumption that an activity is desirable just because it is legal. The law allows a large number of activities (such as gambling) which, in the view of many people, ought not to be encouraged.

4. Would Legalisation Get Criminals Out of Drugs?

Drug traders would cease to be criminals by definition. Some drug production and distribution might remain in the same hands following legalisation. As in other markets, there might be cases of unsavoury business practices. But the trade would be subject to taxation and the same laws of fair trading and product liability as any other business.

It might be feared that the Medellin cartel and other large criminal firms would use terror and corruption to establish monopolies not dissimilar to those which exist in the illegal market. This might be feasible within a single country, but legalisation would open the market to international competition from law-abiding firms and this makes it most improbable that an international cartel could be effective.

Cartels depend for their success on limiting supply by agreeing quotas amongst the membership. Quotas must be enforceable, and the cartel must therefore control a high proportion of the world supply of the commodity. In the production of drugs, both natural and synthetic, there are no scarce factors of production which would constitute a barrier to entry. Quotas would be difficult to enforce and the Third World would face stiff competition from natural and synthetic drugs produced in the West. The Medellin cartel would find that the forces of competition impose a much sterner discipline than does the US Marine Corps.

A separate but related issue concerns the economic impact of legalisation on Third World producers. If drug crops become normal internationally traded products, it is possible but not certain that some Latin American countries would suffer losses in income, employment and foreign exchange. Prices to growers could fall but most of the value of drugs in

---

5 Rt. Hon. Douglas Hurd, MP, *op. cit.*

the illegal market is added at the distribution stage. Farm prices would therefore probably fall by much less than retail prices. Production costs would also fall since clandestine production under the threat of crop seizure cannot be efficient. Profitability, however, would depend on competitiveness with natural and synthetic drugs produced elsewhere in the world. In the face of so many variables which include the size of the legal market, the total effect of legalisation on farm incomes is imponderable.

In a Labour Party Consultation Document, Roy Hattersley, MP, argued that legalisation would

> 'accelerate dangerous tendencies towards mono-cultivation, displacing present patterns of mixed farming ... and displace peasant farmers to make way for big commercial farms, paying low wages'.[6]

Even if this statement is correct in its predictions, it is surely unreasonable to argue that prohibition should be retained as a device to protect peasant farmers from large-scale agri-business. In practice, peasant farmers, caught between criminal dealers and the US Marine Corps, are amongst those groups which suffer most directly from prohibition.

Legalisation could cause hardship in some poor countries, but drug-producing countries stand to gain more than most from the social and political benefits of legalisation. Short-term economic dislocation created by legalisation (if any) could be alleviated from the resources saved by reduced international drug law enforcement.

5. Could the UK Legalise Drugs Unilaterally?

When homosexuality between consenting adults was legalised, it was predicted that London would become 'the capital of queerdom'. Similarly, critics claim that if the UK legalised drugs unilaterally, London would attract enough 'junkies' to wrest from Amsterdam the title 'Drug Capital of the World'.

If the UK was alone in abandoning prohibition, 'drug tourism' might become a nuisance, as it is in Holland. It is

---

6 Roy Hattersley, MP, *Drugs: A Consultation Document*, The Labour Party, June 1991.

unlikely, however, that the UK would remain alone for long. Marco Taradash was elected as an Italian member to the European Parliament on an anti-prohibition ticket; organisations which support drug law reform have supporters throughout the world; and in Europe and Latin America there are clear signs of a movement away from US policies.

This tendency, scarcely detectable in national politicians, is strongest in local government and among people who deal directly with drug problems. In the UK several judges and senior policemen[7] have recognised the need to reform drug laws. A conference of police chiefs, burgomasters and medical officers from large European cities with major drug problems approved a declaration in November 1990 which amounted to a recommendation of decriminalisation. Commenting in an editorial, *The Lancet* said: 'the abject failure of prevailing policies is now so generally acknowledged that the momentum towards decriminalisation is surely becoming unstoppable'.[8]

Decriminalisation is not the same as legalisation but, elsewhere in the world, public health considerations combine with urgent political needs to create an atmosphere in which radical alternatives to current policies are being considered seriously. This was seen in July 1991 when Bolivian farmers clashed with US troops, and the Colombian government reversed its policy of extraditing drug dealers to the USA. Even within the United States there is a groundswell of opinion which favours changes in the law. Most strikingly, the Surgeon-General, Dr Jocelyn Elders, identified the high murder rate (50 per cent of which is drug-related) as a major menace to public health. In December 1993, and again in January 1994, Dr Elders argued that the US administration ought at least to study legalisation as a means of reducing violent crime and other public health risks.[9]

7 For example, Commander John Grieve, head of criminal intelligence at the Metropolitan Police ('Licensing of drugs urged', report in *The Independent*, 14 May 1993), and Edward Ellison, former Central Drug Squad Detective Chief Superintendent (in an article, 'Legalise drugs now: it's the only answer', in *The Daily Telegraph*, 5 October 1993).

8 *The Lancet*, Vol.337, 16 February 1991, p.402.

9 'Legalising Drugs: Another Look', *The Economist*, 22 January 1994.

6. How Do We Protect Children?

All drug law reformers agree that the sale of drugs to minors should remain illegal and that the law should be enforced strictly. It is, however, accepted that this might not be more effective than current restrictions on the sale of cigarettes and alcohol to children.

Critics will seize on this admission as damaging to the whole case for legalisation, but children fare particularly badly under prohibition and, as parents are aware, it is difficult to protect children from hazards of all sorts. Life is a risky business and the prohibition of drugs does not reduce that risk. Indeed, prohibition is positively dangerous to the extent that it creates a demand for that which is forbidden, and implies that substances which are legal must be safe. Children have to learn risk-management, and where education and parental example fail, the forces of the law and the prison service are unlikely to succeed.

Critics have raised legitimate doubts about the consequences of drug legalisation but they have yet to make a convincing case for the continuation of prohibition. It is doubtful whether any such case can be sustained on ethical, social or medical grounds. Prohibition implies a faith in the power of governments to protect citizens and to suppress illegal markets which experience does not support.

VI. LEGALISATION IN PRACTICE

In a legal system it would no longer be an offence to. possess, use or trade in drugs. Under such a régime a variety of institutional arrangements is possible. All legalisation proposals, however, agree that drugs would bear a sternly-worded government health warning and that sales to children would remain illegal. (This much was conceded by John Stuart Mill in 1859.[1])

Legalisation proposals differ mainly in the amount of state intervention envisaged. For example, a French lawyer, Francis Caballero, proposes a state monopoly of production and distribution, and would prohibit advertising or any other form of incitement to consume drugs.[2] In Scandinavia and parts of Canada and the USA where the sale of alcohol is a state monopoly, a similar monopoly for drugs might be the only acceptable approach; otherwise psychoactive drugs would be less strictly controlled than alcohol.

Elsewhere, drugs could be produced and sold in private markets subject to differing degrees of regulation. Joseph Galiber presented a bill to the New York State Senate in 1989 which proposed a private market system regulated by detailed licensing and zoning restrictions.[3] Other supporters of legalisation regard most of the evils of drug abuse as entirely predictable consequences of the failure of government intervention, and would prefer to minimise the rôle of government. In principle, there is no reason why drugs should not be sold in relatively unfettered markets, subject only to existing laws as they apply to most ordinary goods.[4] The next section explains how such a market system might

---

1 J.S. Mill, *On Liberty* (1859), London: Pelican Books, 1974.

2 Francis Caballero, *Droit de la Drogue*, Paris: Dalloz, 1989.

3 J. Galiber, 'A bill to make all drugs as legal as alcohol', in Trebach & Zeese, *op. cit.*

4 Richard Stevenson, 'Can markets cope with drugs?', *Journal of Drug Issues*, Vol.20, No.4, 1990, pp.659-66.

work, but reservations are expressed. Much depends on the nature and performance of legal markets. Circumstances might emerge in which specific drug market regulation would be desirable, but in the meantime there is a case for the exercise of regulatory constraint.

A Free Market in Drugs

After 70 years of prohibition it is difficult to predict the dimensions and nature of a legal market, but the likelihood is that costs and prices would fall, product quality would improve, and private markets would be 'workably competitive'.[5]

In illegal markets, firms are designed to survive penetration by the enforcement agencies and are inefficient by the standards of legal companies.[6] In New York, for example, there is said to be a six-tiered distribution network. Along this chain, information flows are strictly controlled so that the apprehension of a single operator does not compromise the entire network.[7] If modern trends in retailing are a guide, fewer distribution stages would be required in a legal drug industry, and costs would be further reduced by improved information flows within firms. Competition among firms, and the need to comply with product liability law, would ensure improvements in the quality of the product.

In competitive markets, profitability would determine the dominant market form at the retail level. A range of products differentiated by brand name would be offered for sale, and drug users would choose among them in much the same way as drinkers choose between beer, wine and spirits. *In ideal circumstances, the self-interest* of users and producers would *combine* to minimise the dangers of drug use.

Users have a powerful incentive to avoid the health risks inherent in drug use. In many markets where products are highly differentiated, and the consequences of mistakes can be serious (if only financially), consumers find it profitable to

---

5 R.J. Michaels, in Hamowy, *op. cit.*

6 S. Rottenburg, 'The clandestine distribution of heroin, its discovery and suppression', *Journal of Political Economy*, Vol.76, 1968, pp.78-90.

7 M.H. Moore, *Buy and Bust: The Effective Regulation of an Illicit Market in Heroin*, Lexington, Mass.: D.C. Heath and Company, 1977.

invest in market information. Good food guides and *Which?* magazine are examples. Information networks exist in illegal drug markets but, being clandestine, they are highly imperfect. If drugs were legal, information flows would develop in parallel with product markets. Some drug information could be sold, perhaps in magazines, and some would be provided by drug companies and voluntary groups.

The Supply Side

It might be feared that legalisation would lead to a market in which many dealers of doubtful reputation would peddle dangerous substances to the detriment of public health. In fact, such features are more characteristic of illegal than of legal markets. During Prohibition in the USA, adulterated whisky was a threat to health and life. In present-day legal markets, contaminated whisky is unknown. Brand names are amongst the principal assets of companies and product safety is of paramount importance. In general, the self-interest of drug companies might be expected to lead to the orderly marketing of safe products, but much would depend on the structure and performance of the industry at the production, distribution and retailing stages.

At the production level, ample resources and the absence of significant barriers to entry would be likely to produce a competitive international market in which natural drugs competed with synthetic drugs. At the processing and distribution stages, economies of scale might give rise to large companies. They could be new specialist drug firms, or existing companies with complementary interests in tobacco or pharmaceuticals.

Large companies with heavy investment in their corporate images intend to stay in business. Irrespective of the requirements of the law, they have incentives to market safe, carefully labelled and packaged products. Price competition is unlikely to be a strong feature of markets in standard products such as heroin and cocaine. If the experience of pharmaceuticals is a guide, drug products would have a life-cycle over which profitability eventually declined. In competitive environments, corporate profitability depends on continuous innovation, so that new products emerge as existing products reach the declining stages of their life-cycles.

In research and development, and marketing strategies of all sorts, safety considerations would be dominant. One likely effect of legalisation would be to stimulate a search for new sorts of drugs to provide the characteristics which users demand in safer forms.[8] For this reason, it would seem unnecessary and undesirable to restrict the flow of product information arbitrarily by prohibiting advertising. It should not be assumed that it would pay to advertise drugs 'like soap powder'. Advertising allows firms to inform consumers of the existence of weaker or safer drugs like low-tar cigarettes and low-alcohol beer. Sober, informative drug advertising could serve a corporate image as well as the public interest.

Equilibrium in a Free Market

In a market system, equilibrium is approached by an adjustment process. Competitive mechanisms determine the most profitable production and distribution methods and users also follow a learning process. In drugs markets most people would abstain; some would learn to cope; and there would no doubt be casualties. Mistakes would be made and some users would suffer, but private citizens are not helpless in the face of market imperfections. Drug users, and those who care about drug users, would organise in response to drug problems as they do in the illegal market.

Parents, therapeutic communities and other institutions would continue to play important rôles in dealing with problem users. In a legal market, they might well be more effective than at present. Drug users would also band together to protect their interests. On the supply side, some drug production and distribution would be taken up by co-operatives such as those which already exist in California. In the longer term, systems of informal control based on custom, manners and precept might well be established so as to remove or greatly reduce the need for regulation.

Ideally, regulation should flow from demonstrable failings in the market; it is justifiable if, *and only if,* governments can do better. Unless those strict conditions are met, free market legalisers will be reluctant to admit that specific drug market regulation will be beneficial.

---

[8] In Holland plant breeders have already produced improved strains of cannabis illegally.

Regulatory Frameworks

It is feasible for psychoactive drugs to be sold like most ordinary goods, but circumstances might arise in which regulation appeared desirable for efficiency reasons. For instance, the transition from prohibition to an orderly market might be long and bumpy, and regulation could perform a useful function by smoothing the path. Moreover, regulation could be desirable if drug markets performed badly. However, legislators are unlikely to be willing to exercise regulatory restraint until after the performance of drug markets has been demonstrated. In the present climate of opinion, the public would probably require what it regards as safeguards before legalisation can proceed.

Most probably governments would insist on licensing producers and distributors and would control some aspects of marketing strategies. Consideration would be given to legalising some drugs and not others, though such a move should be resisted since it would give an incentive to criminals to specialise in the sale of the more dangerous sorts. More sensibly, government or the industry could standardise purity and packaging to reduce the risk of overdosing.

At the retail level, government might not be content to allow market forces to determine the dominant market form. Sales could be restricted to pharmacists who might be required to give a personal word of warning. A ban on advertising would probably also be proposed. As explained above, a total ban would be a mistake, but no doubt pressure would exist to regulate along the lines adopted for cigarettes and alcohol. It is already an offence to operate a motor vehicle under the influence of drugs, but if drugs were more freely available, drug testing for some occupational groups such as cab drivers and airline pilots might become more commonplace.

Governments could also seek ways of improving the working of the legal market. Education programmes could be a cost-effective means of reducing demands on the NHS, which would continue to provide services for problem users. Legalisation might increase the demand for NHS services, but it would also release resources currently employed in law enforcement. Some proportion of those savings could be devoted to much improved services for problem users.

Legalisation also raises the issue of taxing drugs as a means of raising revenue and restraining demand. There is a case for an 'optimum tax' which would raise just enough revenue to compensate for the costs drug users impose on others, though it would be very difficult to calculate what that rate of tax should be. Since most of the external costs of drug abuse are a consequence of its illegality, an optimum tax might be too small to satisfy either the Exchequer or those who would argue for a high tax to curb demand. It would seem reasonable to tax psychoactive drugs at rates similar to those imposed on tobacco and alcohol, but hard to justify rates which are any higher.

This brief account by no means exhausts the possibilities for government intervention in the legal drug market. It does, however, raise the issue of whether the objectives of legalisation might be compromised by excessive regulation.

The Regulatory Threat

Legalisation without some sort of regulation may well be unattainable but in the political process which determines the nature and extent of that regulation, economists' notions of efficiency receive scant attention. Also under-represented in the debate are those who argue in favour of the freedom to choose. In consequence, the authority of the state is more likely to be invoked on the side of choice restriction. For such reasons, Littlechild and Wiseman have argued that policy proposals which restrict choice should be regarded with 'cautious suspicion'.[9]

The case for regulatory restraint is particularly strong where drugs are concerned because the quality of information available to decision-makers is likely to be of poor quality. Hamowy has shown that in the United States, private and public interest groups have consistently resorted to misrepresentation in pursuit of their objectives.[10] Reference has been made to popular misconceptions of the nature of drug abuse (Chapter II) and even British Ministers are prone to sensational and inaccurate statements (Chapter III, p. 42).

---

9 S.C. Littlechild and J. Wiseman, 'The political economy of the restriction of choice', *Public Choice*, Vol.51, 1986, pp.161-72.

10 R. Hamowy, 'Illicit drugs and government control', in Hamowy, *op. cit.*

Moreover, in all countries large bureaucracies have vested interest in exaggerating the perils of drug abuse.

The misinformation which surrounds drug issues biases public opinion in the direction of government control, and government control, as Professor Griffith Edwards has written:

> '..bear[s] witness to a profound distrust of the strength and quality of our own culture. It can then be argued that the process becomes circular, and the more we legislate ... the more certainly will informal cultural processes wither and fade'.[11]

Drug market regulation designed in advance of legalisation attempts to out-guess markets. Premature regulation may lead to allocative and technical inefficiency and cannot guarantee to protect the drug user any more effectively than does prohibition. Some regulation is politically unavoidable, but until markets have had a chance to perform, regulation is best regarded as a threat to be resisted.

Summary and Conclusion

A preference has been expressed in this *Hobart Paper* for a relatively free market system for the production and distribution of drugs. In part this is a response to critics who have claimed (mistakenly) that proponents of legalisation are reticent in matters of operational detail. However, uncertainty about the nature of a legal market militates against dogmatism. It would be sensible to proceed cautiously, to monitor consequences and to revise ideas in response to experience. Institutional arrangements are a matter for debate but they are not a serious impediment to drug law reform.

All legal systems offer economic, social, political and medical advantages over prohibition. The economic case for legalisation is particularly strong. Cheap legal drugs will reduce the external costs of drug use which are found in acquisitive (sometimes violent) crime and risks to public health. Savings can be expected in police forces and the criminal justice system. In the private sector, a reduction in crime will cut the cost of protecting property.

---

11 V. Berridge and G. Edwards, *op. cit.*, p.261.

It is by no means certain that the consumption of some of the less attractive substances such as heroin will increase. This has not, for instance, been the experience of The Netherlands. The use of some drugs may increase but it does not follow that the number of problem users will also rise. Drug use in illegal markets is peculiarly dangerous. In legal markets, assured product quality will reduce these dangers.

It is not supposed that legalisation will solve all drug problems but the problems which remain will be social and medical. Legalisers believe that individual users, their families, voluntary agencies and the medical profession will cope better in a legal system where problems are visible. It might also be hoped that some part of the resources currently devoted to the enforcement of laws which are unenforceable might be directed to helping problem users who fare so badly under prohibition.

Commentaries

1.

A Short History of Narcotic Addiction and the Case for Regulated Legalisation

by

JULIUS MERRY

2.

The Non-Case for Legalisation

by

PETER REUTER
MICHAEL FARRELL
JOHN STRANG

COMMENTARY 1

A SHORT HISTORY OF NARCOTIC
ADDICTION AND THE CASE FOR
REGULATED LEGALISATION

Richard Stevenson's *Hobart Paper* provides a balanced and wide-ranging discussion of drug problems and their management. Stevenson supports drug legalisation and gives cogent reasons for his conclusion.

The problem is an old one. In about 1680 the English physician Thomas Sydenham wrote:

'Among the remedies which it has pleased Almighty God to give to man to relieve his sufferings, none is so universal and so efficacious as opium.'[1]

Some 240 years later, in 1909, S. Hiller stated:

'In these days of "strenuous life" with its consequent strain and worry, most of us are interested in discussion upon the moderate and immoderate use of drugs. The interest is aroused, not only on account of the many people who now treat themselves for their various aches and pains, but also because there are so many instances of the drug habit, that the baneful influence of excess is often apparent to us in a most realistic and painful manner.'[2]

More recently, according to Aldous Huxley in 1959.

'That humanity at large will ever be able to dispense with Artificial Paradises seems very unlikely. Most men and women lead lives at the worst so painful, at the best so monotonous, poor and limited that the urge to escape, the longing to transcend themselves if only for a few moments, is and has always been one of the principal appetites of the soul. Art and religion, carnivals

---

[1] T. Sydenham (1680), quoted from D.R. Laurence, *Clinical Pharmacology*, 3rd edition, London: J. and A. Churchill, 1966, p.224.

[2] S. Hiller, *Popular Drugs – their use and abuse*, London: T. Werner Laurie, 1909, p.9.

and saturnalia, dancing and listening to oratory – all these have served, in H.G. Wells's phrase, as "doors in the wall".'[3]

For private, everyday use there have always been chemical intoxicants. All the vegetable sedatives and narcotics, all the euphorics that grow on trees, the hallucinogens that ripen in berries or can be squeezed from roots – all have been known and systematically used by human beings from time immemorial. To these natural modifiers of consciousness, modern science has added its quota of synthetics – chloral, for example, and benzedrine, the bromides, and the barbiturates.

Most of these modifiers of consciousness cannot now be taken except under doctor's orders, or else illegally and at considerable risk. For unrestricted use the West has permitted only alcohol and tobacco. All the other chemical 'doors in the wall' are labelled 'dope' and their unauthorised takers 'fiends'.

Drugs as Big Business

Richard Stevenson writes of the drug trade as 'one of the world's most valuable and profitable traded goods'. On the same subject, in 1989, Dr Vernon Coleman wrote:

> 'The world trade in illegal drugs is estimated at $500 billion a year. Cocaine dealers in America are said to have made tax-free profits of more than $95 billion last year. Cocaine is now widely recognised as the most profitable traded item in the world...'

> '...This year the relatively small group of criminals who now control illegal drugs will have a bigger turnover than the income of 150 of the world's 170 nations.'[4]

These references stimulated in me a feeling of *déjà vu* because the opium trade in the 18th and 19th centuries formed the basis of large fortunes made by the British (and French) merchant classes. The profits of the opium trade financed great country houses, new banks, cotton mills, coal mines and great college libraries.

---

3 Aldous Huxley, *The Doors of Perception and Heaven and Hell*, London: Penguin Books, 1959, pp.51-52.

4 V. Coleman, *Drugs: The Argument for Decriminalisation*, Committee for a Free Britain, 1989, pp.1 and 4.

China and the Opium Trade

China was the first country where opium presented a social problem. Opium was known in Asia Minor 6,000 years ago; knowledge of the opium poppy spread to Europe and, in the 8th century, to India and China.[5] For more than 1,000 years after its introduction into China by the Arabs, opium was used solely for medicinal purposes, for example for the treatment of malaria and dysentery. A turning point came, however, in the 17th century when tobacco smoking was introduced to the Far East, leading to the mixing of tobacco with opium for smoking purposes. The combination was used to combat various tropical diseases. However, the enhanced pleasurable effect of adding opium to tobacco soon became apparent, resulting predictably in the smoking of opium by itself.

By the year 1729, opium smoking was so widespread that an Imperial Edict was issued forbidding it. The Edict was not at all effective. The East India Company, which was controlled by British merchants, had acquired control of the opium monopoly from the Dutch in 1781 and they then intensified the smuggling of opium into China. In the year 1800, a second Imperial Edict was issued, prohibiting the cultivation and the import of opium into China. This Edict was ignored by the East India Company, which continued to smuggle vast quantities of opium into China. As a consequence, Indian ships were inspected for contraband and there were armed clashes between smugglers and the Chinese authorities.

In 1839 the Chinese government confiscated 20,000 chests of opium; this act resulted in the opium war between England and China. After the British victory in the First Opium War (1839-42), the Chinese ceded Hong Kong to the British (who had occupied it in 1841). The British went on to increase the opium trade and, as a consequence, the Second Opium War (1856-60) took place. The Chinese government was forced to legalise the opium trade and the second victory resulted in the cession of Kowloon and the treaty ports to the British.

---

5 L. Lewin, *Phantastica*, London: Routledge & Kegan Paul, 1964, pp.247, 260, 268.

In view of the high cost of imported opium, China began domestic production. By the year 1900 it was producing six times as much opium as it was importing from India. It was estimated that, by 1906, 20 per cent of the adult Chinese population was smoking opium periodically, and 40 million were said to be addicted to opium smoking. To add to this misery, England, France, Germany and Switzerland shipped huge quantities of heroin and morphine into China. By 1906 the opium menace was so serious that a 10-year prohibition plan was introduced by the government.

Embarrassed by public opinion at home, the British government agreed at the International Opium Convention held at The Hague in 1912 to restrict and later halt the export of opium to China. Meanwhile, the stringent prohibitive controls of the Chinese government and the drastic penalties, including beheading, all but wiped out the habit.

Between 1917 and 1934, however, with the decline of authority of the central government in China, the Regional Governors and corrupt War Lords encouraged the drug traffic and recultivation. Moreover, Chinese labourers and traders carried the opium habit with them when they emigrated to other parts of the Far East – for example, Formosa, Korea, Indo-China and Macao.

Spread of Opium as a Therapeutic Agent in America

In 18th-century America, opium was used by physicians as a therapeutic agent: to relieve pain in cancer and VD, for diarrhoea and vomiting, for the spasms of tetanus, and even for the pain of menstruation and childbirth. But the addictive properties of opium were not understood and society's attitude to opium was comparable to that held for alcohol: indeed, opium was one of the recommended cures for alcoholism. Opium-containing mixtures were indiscriminately distributed by medicinal prescriptions and in patent medicines. However, towards the end of the 18th century some American physicians had come to recognise the opium habit as a problem.[6]

In 1805 the alkaloids, morphine and codeine, were isolated from opium. At that time, morphine was as

---

6 E.M. Schur, *Narcotic Addiction in Britain and America*, London: Tavistock Publications, 1962.

misunderstood as opium had been, in terms of its addictive properties. Indeed, morphine was used to cure the opium habit, with the result that opium addicts were transferred from one addictive drug to another. Moreover, since morphine has about 10 times more euphoriant effect than the equivalent weight of opium, its popularity as a treatment, was assured.

Perhaps the most important factor influencing the spread of narcotic addiction was the invention of the hypodermic needle in 1843. It was brought to North America in 1856 and was extensively used in the Civil War to administer morphine to the battle-wounded and to sufferers from dysentery. Consequently, vast numbers of soldiers were returned to civilian life addicted to morphine. For that reason the addiction was sometimes called the 'Soldiers' Disease'.[7]

Besides injection, opiate abuse in North America took other routes. Opium smoking had been introduced to the large cities of the Pacific and Atlantic coasts by Chinese immigrants. The habit was adopted by non-Chinese and became something of a fashion in the 1920s. There was also widespread use of opium in the form of laudanum and paregoric (mixtures of opium and alcohol), which were popular for the treatment of coughs, diarrhoea and pain. Abuse of opiates was not approved but it was not considered criminal or monstrous; it was rather looked upon as a vice or personal misfortune – much as alcoholism is regarded today.

1898: Heroin Synthesised from Morphine

The final landmark in the development of narcotic addiction is the year 1898, when heroin was synthesised from morphine. Again the addictive nature of the new drug was not recognised and it became the prime treatment for morphine addiction. Heroin also became available in many pharmaceutical preparations and finally established the hypodermic needle as the instrument of drug abuse. During the 1930s, heroin was self-administered by subcutaneous injection. The typical addict used to mix one part of heroin with two parts of lactose (milk sugar). During the Second World War, pure heroin became scarce and was even more

---

7 Office of Health Economics, *Drug Addiction*, London: OHE, 1967.

[77]

heavily diluted with lactose; hence addicts began to inject themselves intravenously in order to obtain maximum effect.[8]

Growth of Drug Abuse Since 1967 Act

Richard Stevenson's paper is concerned with the international trade in heroin, cocaine and cannabis and the more national trades in amphetamines, LSD and ecstasy. Up to the mid-1960s, the illegal trade in and use of heroin had largely occupied centre stage in the debate on the management of drug addiction. But, since the Dangerous Drugs Act of 1967, the abuse of drugs has become more widespread, not only in the variety of drugs (for example, amphetamines, cocaine, LSD, ecstasy, cannabis, solvents) but also in the number of abusers.

The Misuse of Drugs Act 1971, which consolidated earlier legislation based on the 1926 reports by the Rolleston Committee,[9] governs the prescription of drugs, and among other things lays down the following conditions/controls:

O Compulsory notification of addicts to the Home Office;

O Limitation to specially licensed doctors of the prescription of heroin and cocaine to addicts; and

O The establishment of special clinics for drug addicts.

The vast majority of these clinics do not prescribe heroin or cocaine. Instead, they prescribe methadone on a maintenance basis or for a restricted time (that is, a programme which tails to zero).

In response, addicts have sought to avoid the restrictions imposed by the Misuse of Drugs Act on the drug of their preference, usually heroin. Many drug addicts supplement their clinic supply from the black market and other addicts avoid the clinics completely and rely entirely on the black market. To finance black market supplies, it is often necessary to indulge in stealing, burglary, dealing and

---

8 J. Merry, 'A Social History of Heroin Addiction', *British Journal of Addiction*, Vol.70, 1975, pp.307-10.

9 Ministry of Health, *Departmental Committee on Morphine and Heroin Addiction* (Rolleston Committee), London : HMSO, 1926.

prostitution (homosexual and heterosexual).[10] A recent police report stated that the purpose of a large proportion of crime was to finance a drug habit.[11]

The 'War on Drugs'

Richard Stevenson rehearses fairly the arguments in favour of the present 'war on drugs' as well as the arguments in favour of legalisation of drugs. There is no doubt that social factors, such as persistent unemployment of young people and the decay of city centres, provide a fertile soil for addiction in a society with such technological potential that expectations are of abundance. A leading article in *The Lancet* discussed Griffith Edwards's Upjohn Lecture. It reports Professor Edwards (Professor of Addictive Behaviour, University of London) as being

> 'convinced that rearing young people to unemployment and in failing cities has much to do with drug abuse. Breeding people to frustration or sheer hopeless passivity, he said, puts society at risk of heroin or glue or any one of a dozen other chemical manifestations of a society "gone wrong". And he puts the heroin challenge squarely on the politicians. If they get the social and political job wrong, then no amount of customs officers, police enforcement, consultant sessions, or lecturing to school children will be able to pick up the broken pieces.'[12]

The 'war on drugs' has failed to deal with the drugs problem. One pointer to the way in which the problem might be managed is the way society has coped with tobacco (and alcohol) and come to some accommodation with them. Tobacco smoking, for instance, was widely proscribed until the late 18th century. Until then a German smoker would be fined, a Russian smoker would be exiled, and an Italian smoker excommunicated. Today tobacco smoking is not encouraged in Western industrialised countries but there are no longer such drastic penalties. Despite the profits to be

---

10 C. Fazey, 'How do we get addicts off the hook?', *Daily Telegraph*, 7 May 1984, p.16.

11 G. Payne, 'Why drugs must be made legal', *Police Review*, 28 February 1992, pp.388-89.

12 'The Challenge of Addiction', *Lancet*, 1984, Vol.2, pp.1,019-20.

made from tobacco, in Western industrialised countries there has been a reduction in tobacco consumption, largely because of public education.

Drug Profits and Social Attitudes

There is no disagreement that the profit motive is the prime mover in the drug trade. If Richard Stevenson is correct in his analysis that legalisation of drugs would take the profit out of drug trading, then public opinion would support legalisation as likely to lessen the drug problem.

Social attitudes do change and so does legislation, which has adjusted to the tremendous changes of the last 20 years or so. Ten per cent of marriages are now dissolved within two years compared with 1·5 per cent 10 years ago. About a half of all couples now live together before marrying compared with only one-tenth in the early 1960s. In the early 1950s the proportion of births outside marriage was 4·5 per cent. By 1990 it had reached 28 per cent. Laws governing divorce and related matters have adapted to these social changes.

If one looks back at what in previous times seemed immutable – for example, the Divine Right of Kings (which lost its hold after the suppression of the 1745 rebellion in England), the Abolition of the Slave Trade in 1807 [13] (before then thought of as a natural phenomenon destined to continue for ever), or in today's terms, the ordination of women priests in the Church of England – one is encouraged to anticipate a change of attitude to the management of drug addiction.

In the current debate, doctors are divided. There are no hard facts to inform the debate – only educated guesses as to the exact size of the problem and as to what would happen if a form of legalisation was established. Would there be a change in the size or the nature of the drug problem? The answers to such questions can only be conjectural.

Already the discussion of changes in the law regarding drugs is being overtaken by events. Thus the Cheshire Police Force now does not charge persons with possession of small

---

[13] The Act received the Royal Assent on the 25th March. Illegal slave trading continued for some time. An Act of 1811 making it punishable by transportation (a subsequent Act made it a capital offence) finally brought the slave trade to an end.

amounts of drugs but counsels them to enter a treatment programme. Hammersmith and Fulham Police Force adopts a similar strategy and refers users to GPs and drug clinics. Liverpool Police Force cautions persons who are first-time possessors of small amounts and refers them for medical guidance. These police forces have noted a large reduction in crime involvement in those cautioned and referred on to drug-support schemes, compared with the preceding period when, in similar circumstances, users were charged and convicted. Similar findings of reduced criminality have been reported in New York for those addicts referred on to treatment rather than being charged and directed into the legal system.[14]

In April 1992, the South Yorkshire Police Force declared a three-month amnesty on the possession of drugs and invited users to bring in drugs and seek help. This amnesty was established after consultation with the Sheffield Crown Prosecution Service and in effect involved a suspension of the law: thus it was a temporary decriminalisation. The underlying reason given for the amnesty was that it threw out a lifeline of help to the addict rather than the prospect of punishment and rejection.

The Logic of Regulated Legalisation

Events are, as always, moving ahead of legislation. It is clear that the 'war on drugs' has failed. It is now time to accept the logic of some form of legalisation – possibly similar to the legal position on tobacco and alcohol, with additional recommendations similar to those in the Rolleston Report [15]

Briefly, those recommendations were that doctors could prescribe heroin (and morphine) for addicts if it enabled them to lead a useful and reasonably normal life or if it was necessary to treat serious withdrawal symptoms. Thus GPs and hospital consultants could identify heroin addicts. This programme would include the addict being directed to a state shop/pharmacy in order to collect prescribed heroin which was subject to the same quality control, retailing and packaging as for tobacco.

14 BBC Radio 4, *Kaleidoscope*, 1992.

15 *Departmental Committee on Morphine and Heroin Addiction, op. cit.*

US Alcohol Prohibition Legislation
and the Drugs Problem

The drugs problem is far more serious in the United States than in Britain. A partial explanation of this is the consequence of the 18th Amendment passed by the American Senate in 1917 prohibiting the production, transport or sale of alcohol. Prohibition failed còmpletely despite the efforts of the law enforcement agencies. In 1933 the 21st Amendment was passed permitting the legal sale of alcohol. But by then unlawful, efficient and nation-wide organisations had been established by the criminal bootleggers. It was a predictable move for these powerful and wealthy organisations to switch their activities to importing and selling drugs.

There is a lesson to be learned from the failure and the consequences of Prohibition. After Prohibition ended in the United States, production and consumption of alcohol fell by 60 per cent. Could just taking the illegality out of drugs result in a similar drop in their use, because 'forbidden fruits' act as an attraction to some vulnerable people?

There is no hard evidence that legalisation would reduce the size of the drug problem. But legalisation would certainly dramatically reduce illegal profits from drugs and would undoubtedly reduce criminal involvement. It would also ensure that addicts received quality-controlled heroin without feeling that they were being forced to indulge in criminal or anti-social activities. Support for legalisation of drugs is not to be interpreted as encouraging drug use/abuse. Proponents of drugs legalisation wish to see the same attention to the control of manufacture, distribution and sale that already apply to alcohol and tobacco, through new legislation. They also wish to see increasing activity and resources directed to the education of the public – especially young people – in the pernicious and serious dangers of all drugs, including alcohol and tobacco.

JULIUS MERRY
Visiting Professor of Clinical Psychiatry, University of Surrey;
Hon. Physician in Psychological Medicine,
St. Thomas's Hospital, London

COMMENTARY 2

THE NON-CASE FOR LEGALISATION

One of the pleasures (or frustrations) of the debate about drug legalisation is that precious little useful data are available. The analyst can then indulge his or her own preference, providing selective support for that position from a meagre array of ambiguous observations.

Frequently in the legalisation debate, under the guise of an evenhanded treatment of legalisation and its alternatives, prohibition, in all its varieties, is damned by gloomy prognostications about what can be attained, emphasising primarily its current failure to prevent the generation of large criminal profits. Legalisation, a highly theoretical world, is then depicted in rosy terms, with just enough listing of potential problems (all of which turn out to be soluble) to suggest a judicious weighing of pros and cons. Intermediate policy alternatives – the kinds that we think most sensible – are damned for their vagueness.

The matter of drug control is far more complicated than Richard Stevenson's analysis suggests. Consequently we are more than doubtful whether legalisation would in fact be a net benefit to society. Current policies are certainly not optimal but the risks associated with legalisation are immense and the gains far too speculative to justify such a dramatic change. Nor are the achievements of the harm reduction form of prohibition negligible.

We limit our commentary on Stevenson's paper to his selectivity in assessing the magnitude and source of current harms and the likely impact of changes in behaviour if prohibitions were removed. We then add a few words of our own about intermediate alternatives and how the legalisation debate should be viewed at this stage.

The Current Situation

Given that the primary arguments for legalisation are now pragmatic rather than ideological, numbers play a central rôle. Estimates both of the scale of the current problems and (even more importantly) of how these might change under legalisation are at the heart of the issue. Stevenson presents few numbers (sometimes without documentation), interprets them oddly, and then allows himself to make bold quantitative assertions without any figures at all.

For example, the claim of 40 million heroin addicts world-wide is close to an order of magnitude too high;[1] even including opium addicts the number is unlikely to reach over 10 million. The 40 million figure is offered as evidence that the purveyors of illicit drugs have been peculiarly successful in peddling their wares. The number is equally consistent with claims that heroin is a highly attractive drug, particularly for those whose lives are otherwise fairly bleak (a disturbingly frequent condition), and that it might be much increased if the drugs were legally available.

The overstatement of numbers is paralleled by exaggeration in conclusions. '[S]upply-side policies have made no discernible impact on the global availability of drugs' (p.33) goes well beyond the conclusion of any serious analysis and indeed contradicts much of Stevenson's own argument. It is certainly true that in Burma (opium) and Peru (coca), peasants produce drugs with scarcely a worry about the activities of the local gendarmerie or military. But the very high price of heroin in the United Kingdom and the United States (though it has important negative consequences in terms of crime and health of addicts), and the difficulty of obtaining the drug in most communities, are tributes to the impact of supply-side policies.[2]

---

1 Stevenson offers no documentation for the claimed 40 million heroin addicts. Taking the conventional (and often inflated) estimates for the United States (750,000), Western Europe (1 million?), Iran (1 million), Pakistan (1.5 million) and Thailand (1 million), we can get a total of 5-6 million; perhaps another million can be found in Hong Kong, Malaysia and Laos. There may be a similar number of opium addicts, primarily in China, Iran, Pakistan and Thailand. These are not trivial numbers but they leave us far from the 40 million claim.

2 For example, through most of the 1980s less than 25 per cent of American high school seniors reported in 1991 that heroin was available to them, compared to about 90 per cent reporting marijuana as available: see L. Johnston, J. Bachman and P. O'Malley, *Smoking, Drinking and Illicit Drug Use Among Secondary Students, College Students, and Young Adults, 1975-1991*, Rockville, MD: National Institute on Drug Abuse, 1992.

Stevenson believes that the fact that one-third of young people have used an illegal drug (p.20) points to the unenforceability of drug prohibition; in fact, over one-half of young people have violated other more serious laws, a finding which indeed points to the difficulty of constraining behaviour with criminal prohibitions but does not speak clearly to the desirability of retaining those prohibitions on larceny and assault.

Health and Behavioural Consequences

Stevenson is particularly selective in his statements about the consequences of drug use. At times, drugs are given an unreasonably benign image, at others their dangers are exaggerated, depending on which turns out to be more useful to his argument.

'Heavy cocaine users are prone to psychological and behavioural disorders which force them to abstain. It is rare for a person to be addicted for more than two or three years, although a Cheshire woman was maintained in good health on cocaine for 55 years' (p.26).

No doubt the rhetoric of US officials about the dangers of cocaine use is highly exaggerated, but that is not to say that the phenomenon of cocaine dependence is not real or widespread. Responsible estimates suggest that 1·5 million persons are currently cocaine dependent in the United States.[3] Their dependence is of a more complex kind than that found among heroin addicts; cocaine is positively reinforcing, so that in contrast to heroin, the first dose of the day is the least, rather than the most, attractive.[4] Hence those who are cocaine dependent are liable to 'binges'; moreover, the dependence is not physiological but only psychological.

---

3 W. Rhodes, 'Synthetic Estimation Applied to the Prevalence of Drug Use', *Journal of Drug Issues*, Vol.23, No.2, Spring 1993, pp.297-322, estimates 2 million weekly cocaine users; 75 per cent of that is a generous estimate of the fraction that are dependent.

4 Interesting evidence of the market effects of this can be found in data from the Zurich Platzspitz, where for some years, the Zurich government tolerated the retailing and consumption of illicit drugs. At the end of the night the price of heroin declined, as dealers tried to get rid of their wares before the park closed; in contrast, the price of cocaine rose as desperate users sought still another dose before their supply was cut off.

That has therapeutic and medical implications but it is not clear that it is of any significance for policy choices; a substantial percentage of those who use cocaine frequently become dependent and have great difficulty in attaining long-term abstinence. At least five years after the peak of the epidemic of cocaine initiation in the United States there is little evidence that most of those who became dependent in the mid- to late-1980s have managed to give up the habit.[5]

Predicting Change

'If some people insist on using drugs, it is better that they should buy them from law-abiding businessmen than from criminals and better still if they can be integrated into society and brought under medical supervision if it is needed' (p.14). This proposition typifies the problems presented by Stevenson's analysis; the trick is all in the word 'some'. The sentence glides over the point that constantly bedevils discussions of legalisation, namely the extent to which the demand for psychoactive drugs would increase under legalisation. If it were the case, as this sentence suggests, that the only difference between legalisation and prohibition were the circumstances under which a fixed number of users would obtain and use their drugs, the debate would indeed seem silly; but of course that is not the case. There is, as Stevenson later admits, some reason to believe that 'some' might become a much larger number.

But Stevenson cleverly elides this issue of expanded consumption by imposing a peculiar standard on the level of increase with which we should be concerned. Would demand for currently illicit psychoactives approach that for tobacco and alcohol? He (quite reasonably) suggests that only cannabis is ever likely to be as widely used as those two substances.

Let us consider, however, the consequences of heroin consumption reaching levels only one-quarter as high as that for alcohol. In the United States it is estimated that 100

---

5 S. Everingham and P. Rydell, 'Modeling the Demand for Cocaine', Santa Monica, CA: RAND (forthcoming), develop a simulation model reflecting a variety of epidemiological data and find that even if there are no new frequent cocaine users, the number of frequent cocaine users in the USA would decline by only about 50 per cent in the next 15 years.

million adults drink at least once in the course of the year and that 15 per cent of those who drink suffer long-term serious problems as a consequence. If one-quarter as many used heroin and a similar percentage suffered long-term harms, then instead of an estimated 750,000 heroin addicts, the USA would have 9,750,000 experiencing serious problems. Clearly the harm per addict would be less but who would be confident that the harm would be only one-fifth as much? Moreover, it is quite plausible that the 'capture rate' for heroin (that is, the proportion of occasional users who become habitual) would be closer to that for tobacco (over 50 per cent) than that for alcohol.

Stevenson's treatment of the impact of legalisation on drug-related crime is similarly selective. The relationship of crime to drug use is one of the better explored topics in this whole dismal field of drug research. Stevenson correctly notes that cheap drugs would reduce the incentives for acquisitive crime. However, that is only one of three kinds of crime related to drug use;[6] one of the others is the psychoactive effect of drugs themselves. Psychoactive drugs free persons from their inhibitions, or can (particularly stimulants) lead to heightened aggression. Alcohol is involved in as many crimes of violence in the United States as are all the illicits together. A much expanded user base might lead to more crime, though of a different kind from that found under current prohibitions. We do not share Stevenson's assumption that the norms of use for the drugs when legal would be such as greatly to reduce the extent of damage experienced as a result; Western society's experience with alcohol is not reassuring in that respect.

Rush to Judgement

Reasonable people can differ about the appropriate method of regulating the distribution of psychoactive drugs; there are grounds for debate. That debate involves both value-judgements (for instance, how much do we care about the extent to which others are intoxicated or able to avoid dealing with social and psychological responsibilities?) and empirical issues (for example, how many persons would use

---

6 P. Goldstein, 'The Drugs/Violence Nexus: A Tripartite Conceptual Framework', *Journal of Drug Issues*, Vol.14, 1986, pp.493-506.

cocaine if it were legally available and what fraction of them would become dependent?). As we said initially, there is far too much uncertainty about the latter to permit sharp judgements; Stevenson, notwithstanding our critiques of his numbers, assertions and logic, may be correct. But the confidence interval (to use rather loosely a common statistical term) around those numbers and assertions is clearly high enough to give pause.

It is the irreversibility of legalisation that gives particular pause. The failure of alcohol prohibition points to the difficulty of stuffing the genie back into the bottle, if the reader will forgive a bad pun. Long-term use of alcohol was well established in American society and the law, however well intended, failed to deal with that commitment of the population. A few years of legalisation, if indeed it did turn out to produce a large number of abusers of psychoactive drugs, would immensely complicate the task of re-establishing prohibition.[7]

The response to that is to note that current prohibitions continue to wreak their damage and that we must weigh not only uncertainties but also that continued damage. If the effluxion of time were likely to increase our knowledge substantially, then we might take that continued cost with equanimity, in the expectation that society could make a better-informed decision later. Alas, there is little reason to believe that time will provide much more relevant experience for analysis. There are no legalisation experiments (natural or otherwise) currently going on and it turns out to be difficult to extrapolate from differences in the enforcement of prohibitions to the consequences of legalisation.[8] We may develop better estimates of the costs of current prohibitions, more understanding of the relationship between drug use and various health and social problems, and even a clearer conceptualisation of how to weigh the different factors. But

---

7 It is worth noting that the experience of legal cocaine in the USA from 1885 to 1915 turned out to present only modest problems of reversibility. But it is also true that the drug was available in less potent and attractive forms than it is now and that it never had a very large base of recreational users. (See D. Musto, 'Opium, Cocaine and Marijuana in American History', *Scientific American*, July 1991.)

8 R. MacCoun, 'Drugs and the Law: A Psychological Analysis of Drug Prohibition', *Psychological Bulletin*, Vol.113, No.3, 1993, pp.497-512.

the basic empirical issues that might allow a much better-informed decision seem to be beyond reach.

The Alternatives

In light of that, we suggest that more consideration should be given to those alternatives that lie between tough prohibition and legalisation. Stevenson mentions that there are indeed such policies. He concedes that they might improve matters over the current position but that they inevitably drift to decriminalisation, which confers few advantages relative to legalisation. We believe that is far too dismissive a treatment and that many of the current costs associated with drug abuse can be substantially ameliorated without moving to risky legalisation.

Harm reduction, the slogan of much European current drug policy, represents an effort to maintain the deterrent effect of criminal sanctions on decisions to use drugs, while trying to minimise the damage that drug abuse does to those who become frequent users. It accepts, at least implicitly, the possibility of a trade-off between increasing the number of drug users and reducing the total harm generated by their use. Needle exchange is the classic example. Perhaps making new needles accessible to intravenous drug users lengthens heroin-using careers and lessens the clarity of government anti-drug messages. But the more substantial and probable gains in slowing the spread of HIV seem well worth that risk. An increasing number of European governments, though by no means all,[9] has come to accept that proposition.

Harm reduction, however, goes far beyond needle exchange. It can affect police tactics. For example, police may choose not to attack orderly drug markets that service only experienced users but to go only after disorderly markets or ones which provide drugs to new users. Sentencing, which in many countries is now dominated by the weight of drugs (including adulterants), can be structured to reflect more precisely the gravity of the offence involved. There is almost no dimension of drug policy that

---

9 The Norwegian and Swedish governments have explicitly rejected this move. In the United States the House of Representatives has passed legislation that continues the ban on federal funds for needle exchange schemes, even including research on the topic.

cannot be improved so as to reduce the harms arising from drug prohibition.

That is not to say that harm reduction can enormously reduce the damage drugs do to individuals and society. Even with more sensible enforcement, illegal drugs will be substantially more expensive than they would be if legal and will be sold with dangerous adulterants. But if the choice is between prohibition and the speculative gains of legalisation, we suggest that more thought about how to reduce the costs of prohibition is what ought to take precedence on a realistic policy research agenda.

PETER REUTER
Department of Criminology, University of Maryland

MICHAEL FARRELL
National Addiction Centre, Institute of Psychiatry, London

JOHN STRANG
National Addiction Centre, Institute of Psychiatry, London

QUESTIONS AND TOPICS
FOR DISCUSSION

1. Should public policy concern itself with psychoactive drugs?

2. Under which circumstances is supply-side drug law enforcement likely to be most effective in reducing drug use?

3. 'Current drug policy is expensive to enforce and damages those most in need of protection'. Do you agree?

4. Why do approximately 90 per cent of habitual drug users prefer low-quality, expensive street drugs to the pure drugs which are available free of charge from the NHS?

5. Distinguish between decriminalisation, legalisation and harm reduction policy.

6. What minimum safeguards would be needed in a legal system for the production and distribution of psychoactive drugs? Should advertising be prohibited?

7. Should legal drugs be taxed? If so, what considerations should enter into the determination of the tax rate? Should it be the same for all drugs?

8. Does it seem likely that legalisation would lead to an increase in consumption? Is this necessarily a matter for concern?

FURTHER READING

Berridge, Virginia, and Griffith Edwards, *Opium and the People: Opiate Use in Nineteenth-Century England*, London: Allen Lane, 1981.

Griffin, Jane, *Drug Misuse*, London: Office of Health Economics, 1992.

Hamowy, Ronald (ed.), *Dealing With Drugs*, Lexington, Mass.: D.C. Heath and Company, 1987.

MacGregor, Susanne (ed.), *Drugs and British Society*, London: Routledge, 1989.

Royal College of Psychiatrists, *Drug Scenes*, London: Gaskell, 1987.

Nadelmann, Ethan A., 'Drug prohibition in the United States: costs, consequences, and the alternatives', *Science*, 1 September 1989, pp.245, 939-47.

Rottenburg, S., 'The Clandestine Distribution of Heroin, Its Discovery and Suppression', *Journal of Political Economy*, Vol.76, 1968, pp.76, 78-90.

Szasz, Thomas S., *Ceremonial Chemistry; The Ritual Persecutions of Drugs, Addicts and Pushers*, Garden City, New York: Doubleday, 1974.

Wagstaff, A., and A. Maynard, *Economic Aspects of the Illicit Drug Market and Drug Enforcement Policies in the United Kingdom*, Home Office Research Study No. 95, London: HMSO, 1988.

Westermeyer, Joseph, 'The Pro-Heroin Effects of Anti-Opium Laws in Asia', *Archives of General Psychiatry*, Vol.33, September 1976, pp.1,135-39.

Zinberg, Norman E., *Drug, Set, and Setting: The Basis for Controlled Intoxicant Use*, New Haven: Yale University Press, 1984.

Economic
Fallacies
Exposed

Geoffrey Wood

Since 1988, Professor Geoffrey Wood of City University
Business School has written a regular column in the
Institute`s journal, Economic Affairs, in which he exposes
popular economic fallacies. Occasional Paper 102 is a
collection of these columns which includes many of the
fallacies in common circulation – for example, about the
supposed dangers of free trade, about the abilities of
governments to control economies, about the significance
of current account deficits, about the use of fiscal policy to
control inflation and about the effects of government
regulation of markets.

These lucid and stimulating columns are invaluable to
students, struggling to master some of the complexities of
economic theory and its applications, who often find that
the most effective way of learning economic analysis is to
see such fallacies exposed. It is a text particularly suitable
for first year University students of economics which
complements existing textbook by using examples to
clarify fundamental concepts in economics and to
demonstrate the practical uses of economic theory.

The Institute of Economic Affairs
2 Lord North Street, Westminster, London SW1P 3LB
Telephone: 0171 799 3745 Facsimile: 0171 799 2137
E-mail: iea@iea.org.uk Internet: http://www.iea.org.uk

ISBN 0-255 36407-5

£8.00

How Markets Work:
Disequilibrium, Entrepreneurship and Discovery

Israel M. Kirzner

1. Mainstream neo-classical economics focusses on already attained states of equilibrium. It is silent about the processes of adjustment to equilibrium.

2. Human action consists of '…grappling with an essentially unknown future', not being confronted with clearly-specified objectives, known resources and defined courses of action as mainstream theory assumes.

3. Critics of the market economy find ammunition in neo-classical theory: they '…merely need to tick off the respects in which real world capitalism departs from the requirements for perfectly competitive optimality'.

4. The theory of entrepreneurial discovery allows economists to escape from the 'analytical box' in which 'choice' simply consists of computing a solution implicit in given data.

5. An entrepreneurial act of discovery consists in '…realising the existence of market value that has hitherto been overlooked'. Scope for entrepreneurial discovery occurs in a world of disequilibrium – which is quite different from the equilibrium world of mainstream economics where market outcomes are foreordained.

6. Entrepreneurial discovery explains why one price tends to prevail in a market. Though new causes of price differences continually appear, entrepreneurs exploit the resulting profit opportunities and produce a tendency towards a single price.

7. Only with the introduction of entrepreneurship is it possible to appreciate how markets work. Without entrepreneurship, there would be no market co-ordination.

8. So-called 'imperfections' of competition are often '…crucial elements in the market process of discovery and correction of earlier entrepreneurial errors'.

9. Advertising expenditures, for example, are means of alerting consumers to 'what they do not know that they do not know'. Anti-trust laws may hamper market processes and prevent competitive entry to markets.

10. Entrepreneurial profit, far from generating injustice, is a 'created gain'. It is not '…sliced from a pre-existing pie…it is a portion which has been created in the very act of grasping it'.

The Institute of Economic Affairs
2 Lord North Street, Westminster, London SW1P 3LB
Telephone: 0171 799 3745 Facsimile: 0171 799 2137
E-mail: iea@iea.org.uk Internet: http://www.iea.org.uk

ISBN 0-255 36404-0

£8.00

Markets in the Firm

A Market-Process Approach to Management

Tyler Cowen and David Parker

1. Information is now the critical factor of production: firms need to be able to sense the need for change and respond before their competitors do.

2. Use of market principles within a firm can help it learn and adapt.

3. The days are numbered when rigid 'Taylorist scientific management' principles could usefully be applied. Markets now demand more variety and quality. Companies are decentralising to cope with the uncertainty and pace of change of markets.

4. 'Looser-coupled' firms, however, run the risk of anarchy. Means of maintaining the 'coherence and strategic direction of the firm' are required.

5. Economists from Ronald Coase onwards have been interested in why firms exist. Viewing the firm as a 'nexus of contracts' focuses attention on the similarities between resource allocation in markets and in firms.

6. Some companies have applied market principles '...to unlock the problems of management.' Koch Industries Inc. in Kansas has been particularly successful.

7. Its success appears to have been achieved by an integrated system of mission statements, decentralised management (profit centres and cross-functional teams), and definition of property rights within the firm so as to provide appropriate incentives.

8. 'Command-and-control' methods are as inappropriate within a firm as they have proved to be outside it. Firms need to harness the ability of markets to 'flex and change, assimilating and processing information speedily and accurately, attributes that are essential to the learning organisation.' (p 73).

9. The 'command firm' is '...subject to all the disincentives of planned economies, including the hiding of resources, aggravated shortages, the over- or under-use of inputs and the resulting inefficiencies of production.' (p78).

10. Market economies have been effective in '...encouraging learning, adaptation and innovation'. The challenge is to '...design firms that can mimic these attributes of the market economy.' (p80).

The Institute of Economic Affairs

2 Lord North Street, Westminster, London SW1P 3LB
Telephone: 0171 799 3745 Facsimile: 0171 799 2137
E-mail: iea@iea.org.uk Internet: http://www.iea.org.uk   ISBN 0-255 36405-9

£8.00

Regulating Utilities: Broadening the Debate

Utility regulation has become not only a major area for academic research but an important economic policy issue.

Every year the Institute, in conjunction with London Business School, publishes a volume of Readings which provides an intellectual foundation for discussions about regulation. It reviews regulatory problems in Britain, considers how they might be solved and draws on experience of other countries. Its authors present a variety of viewpoints in order to stimulate debate about regulatory issues.

The 1997 edition of this comprehensive survey of utility regulation contains comments from the utility regulators and the Director General of Fair Trading as well as from academic commentators and practitioners in the field.

Contents

Introduction

M.E. BEESLEY

The Institute of Economic Affairs

2 Lord North Street, Westminster, London SW1P 3LB
Telephone: 0171 799 3745 Facsimile: 0171 799 2137
E-mail: iea@iea.org.uk Internet: http://www.iea.org.uk

ISBN: 0-255 36406-7

£17.00